B. P. Pratten

La Corte

Letters from Spain, 1863-1866

B. P. Pratten

La Corte
Letters from Spain, 1863-1866

ISBN/EAN: 9783337246198

Printed in Europe, USA, Canada, Australia, Japan

Cover: Foto ©ninafisch / pixelio.de

More available books at **www.hansebooks.com**

LA CORTE.

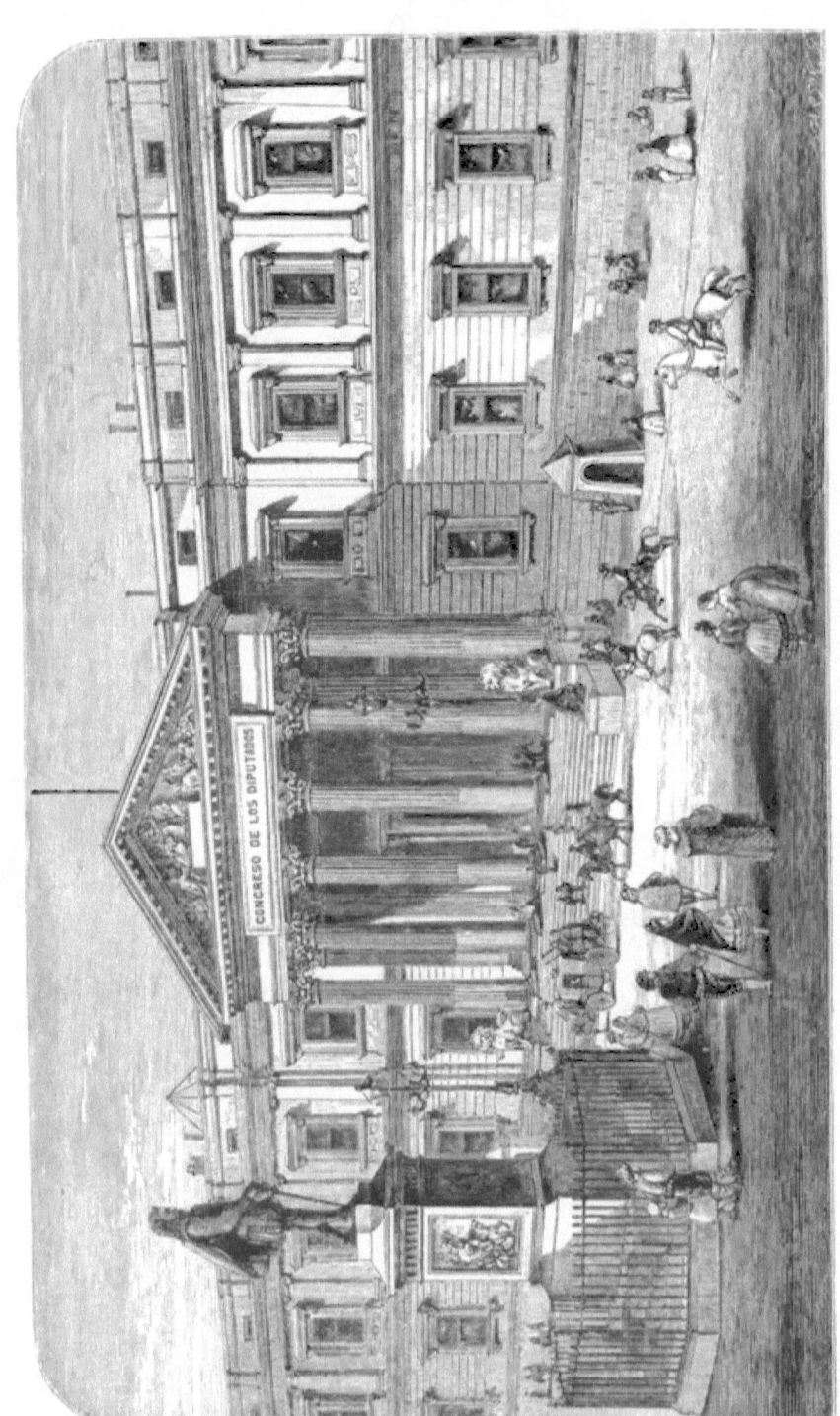

PALACE OF THE CORTES, AND STATUE OF CERVANTES, MADRID.

LA CORTE:

LETTERS FROM SPAIN, 1863 TO 1866.

BY A RESIDENT THERE.

LONDON:
SAUNDERS, OTLEY, AND CO.,
7 (late 66), BROOK STREET, W.
1868.

[*All Rights reserved.*]

PREFACE.

Now that the completion of the railway across the Pyrenees has opened up Spain to the English tourists, and numbers of these enterprising pleasure-seekers find their way every year to the "Capital of the World," as its inhabitants boastfully call Madrid, numerous books have been written professing to give a more or less exhaustive account of Spain and the Spaniards. Looking at those which have been published within the last two years, the question might well be asked, "Why add to their number?" It is believed, however, that these Letters, written originally without the most distant thought of future publication, may give a different view of life in Spain from that which any mere tourist in the country could do.

Without trenching, then, on the ground which Ford's masterly work has thoroughly exhausted, or attempting in any way to undertake the part of cicerone, the writer merely professes to give her own experience of life among the Spaniards in the present day, and her actual impressions of a country to which she went, as most English people do, as to a country of beauty and wonder, over which the pens of Byron and Washington Irving have thrown a halo of romance.

LIST OF ILLUSTRATIONS.

	PAGE
THE PALACE OF THE CORTES, AND STATUE OF CERVANTES, MADRID	*Frontispiece*
BULLOCK DRIVER	25
ASTURIAN NURSE—IN NATIONAL COSTUME	27
PRIEST, WITH HIS GIMLET HAT	28, 32
MANNER OF WEARING THE "CAPA"	39
OLD LADY WEARING THE MANTILLA	40
THE "MODERN VELA"	41
NORIA FOR RAISING WATER	64
HOW SPANIARDS CATCH "PULMONÍA"	81
VALENCIANO IN WINTER COSTUME	93
VALENCIAN, WITH PALMITO	108
SELF AND STEED	109
VALENCIAN VILLAGER INSPECTING THE NEW CURIOSITY	112
HIDALGO IN GALA COSTUME	113
RAILWAY GUARD IN NIGHT COSTUME	117

LIST OF ILLUSTRATIONS.

	PAGE
THE GRACEFUL SPANISH DANCE, AS SEEN IN MADRID	146
ANDALUSIAN DRESS	166
OLD STYLE OF WATERING THE STREETS	204
COUNTRY WOMAN ON HER DONKEY	205
PRIEST	281
DONKEY CARRYING STRAW	293
BULLOCK DRIVER IN WINTER	309

LA CORTE.

LETTER I.

BAYONNE, *September* 26, 1863.

MY DEAR,—We arrived here safely about two o'clock this afternoon; but too late for the English post.

I need not say anything of our stay in Paris, for we only remained there one day, and started for this place at seven o'clock in the evening. Every seat in the carriage was full, and I was the only person who remained awake; but I enjoyed watching the landscape as we whirled rapidly along, past the sleeping towns, which looked picturesque enough in the moonlight. Towards morning I also fell asleep, but awoke in time to see the first commencement of the dawn and watch it stealing gradually over the sky, until almost as the moon sank on one side of the heavens the sun rose on the other, reminding me of Landseer's beautiful picture of the 'Sanctuary:' do you remember it?

Having made my toilet in a furtive way while my fellow-passengers were still sleeping,—for I must confess to having a dislike to be seen in the morning, after travelling all night, until I have done something towards tidying myself,—I had time to look at my companions: and very frowsy I must say they all looked as they began to awake one after another, rub their eyes and shake themselves.

At Bordeaux we were very glad to stop, about seven o'clock, for an hour's rest for breakfast and a good wash, which was an unexpected luxury. I left my rings on the washing-stand, and never missed them until the woman who had charge of the dressing-room brought them to me just as we were starting. On returning to our carriage we found only one of our fellow-travellers was going on with us, a sombre, thin, and pious-looking priest, who never took his eyes off a little book he was studying except to close them and murmur to himself.

I could not help noticing with astonishment the progress his beard had made during the night. He had started from Paris with a chin as smoothly shaven as became so devout a divine, and behold! now it was like a black polishing-brush, and—in default of other amusement—I interested myself in watching its growth during the remainder of our journey, making mental calculations how long it would take to reach, like Aaron's, "even unto the skirts of his garment." At one of the road-side stations a young French couple got in, who were evidently starting on their wedding journey, and who could not wait for their fellow-travellers to go to sleep to begin kissing and cooing in the most interesting way. The priest, however, was too much engrossed with his devotions, and I with a book, to see anything; and Henry was asleep.

From Bordeaux the scenery is dreary in the extreme: mile after mile of utterly flat waste land,

only rendered interesting to me from having read
'Maître Pierre.' I looked for the pine plantations
which were to protect the Landes from the all-
encroaching sand, and pictured to myself Maître
Pierre galloping over the ground on the famous
"cheval gris," with Marinette by his side. I was
much amused also by watching the people walking
about on stilts in the marshy parts; especially one
old woman whom I saw driving a flock of geese:
they were swimming before her, while she contentedly waded after them, holding her petticoats
well out of the water, regardless of appearances.
The little French couple, however, appeared to find
the scenery beautiful, for they only stopped their
amatory duet to assure each other that the view
was "magnifique."

On arriving at Bayonne, about twelve o'clock,
we drove at once to the Hôtel St. Étienne, and,
after an excellent luncheon, we set out for a walk
round the little bay, into which the Adour empties
itself, to a pine wood, which is situated on a hill
commanding a beautiful view of the quaint old
town, with the reach of water in the foreground

and the Pyrenees behind it. We sat on a bench at the edge of the hill under the pines, listening to the ripple of the water below and watching the boats, as they lazily swung round with the tide, until the sun had set and the moon rose opposite us. We had a good three miles between us and the Hotel, but I was not in the least tired. There had been a cold wind in the morning, but it had dropped, and the air was soft and balmy as a June evening in England. I never saw a more beautiful sky; it was all of the most delicate tint of rose, while the little clouds were snowy-white except for a golden edge where the sun had gone down: there was a broad pathway of light from the full moon across the still waters, and the rugged old mountains stood quiet and grey in the far distance.

We dined on our return to the Hotel, and I have left Henry smoking downstairs with Mr. —— while I came to write to you.

We intend driving to Biarritz to-morrow morning, and start by diligence for Madrid, by way of Pampeluna, in the afternoon.

LETTER II.

MADRID, *September* 29.

HENRY wrote a few lines, I think, last night to say we had arrived, for as we had been travelling for twenty-six hours without stopping, and it was quite a new experience for me, I was rather tired when we reached Madrid, and did not feel quite certain whether I was on my head or my heels.

After writing to you the other evening at Bayonne, I could not resist the temptation of sitting on the cushioned seat of my balcony, which was on a level with the tree-tops, looking out over the old town as it lay sleeping in the moonlight, and thinking of the many strange scenes it had witnessed. It is a quaint, interesting old place, though we did not see very much of it, for the following morning (Sunday) we drove to Biarritz, starting about ten o'clock and remaining till one, wandering about the cliffs and sitting watching the waves dashing up against the rocks and sending jets of spray high into the air, and listening to them booming into the caves beneath us. Biarritz is a pretty little place standing on a high cliff in the bend of a small bay. There are, indeed, a series of little bays, with broken, rugged rocks standing out into the sea. In the distance there is a fine view of the mountains on the Spanish coast. The Imperial villa is at some distance from the town, and stands on a little promontory facing towards Spain. It looks rather bare and square now, but will improve, I dare say, when the young trees which are planted all round it are grown up. On leaving the carriage, we strolled through the narrow, steep, little streets of the town until we came out upon a kind of square, overlooking the sea, where we saw what we imagined to be the English church, but on passing it we found three pretty little phaetons with two horses each standing in the shade, and immediately divined that they belonged to the Emperor and Empress, who were probably at their devotions inside the building. Just at that moment the people began to come quietly out of church, and the carriages drew up to the door. We stood on one side, and in a few moments saw the Emperor and Empress come out, take their places in the phaeton, and go off, the Emperor himself driving. The Empress is still very beautiful. She was dressed quite in seaside costume. A plain winsey dress looped up over a bright-coloured, striped petticoat, a pretty little black hat, and a pair of leather gaiters buttoned on above the boot. These last looked rather funny as she drove away in sublime unconsciousness that her crinoline was not behaving as well as it might have done.

We returned to Bayonne to an early dinner, and started in the diligence for Pampeluna at half-past three. I was sorry to leave Bayonne so soon, for it is a pretty, as well as an interesting place. Lying, as it does, at the foot of the Pyrenees, and on the banks of a river with high wooded banks, it must abound in beautiful walks and rides. The people, too, are fresh and good-looking, with a bright, intelligent expression. The servants wear gay-coloured handkerchiefs tied round their heads, which are very becoming to them, and the better class wear pretty little tulle caps with broad strings, and look so beautifully neat and clean.

I am almost afraid to say anything of our drive across the Pyrenees, for the best I could do would seem but a mockery of description. Henry had secured places in the *coupé*, and a very comfortable little place we found it. We started from Bayonne with six horses at full gallop, and passed through the town, which was gayer than usual, as the Emperor was coming to hold a review there at four o'clock, and all the people were out in their best clothes. The road begins at once to ascend, and is very beautiful, winding so that you never see more than a very short distance before you. You know it was my first experience of diligence travelling, and I enjoyed it very much. The horses galloped up-hill and down, and as we sat in our little box with all the windows open, we found it very pleasant. The driver was far above our heads, on a little perch, from whence he carried on a continuous conversation with his horses, which rattled along as if they rather liked their journey, jingling their bells in a sort of time that harmonized with the voice of the invisible driver. As we neared the mountains, the road of course became much steeper and the horses began to flag before we reached the little village where we changed. The second team of eight were very good, and we tore along the road as if we were mad. At one place we came to a village where the road was apparently as steep as a house-side. We pulled up a moment at the foot to rest, and then off again at full gallop, but the horses had been a little over-driven, and halfway up they stopped dead short, and the great lumbering diligence began sliding down again towards the ravine which we had just crossed on a wonderfully narrow bridge. It seemed utterly impossible that the poor tired horses could ever start again, or, indeed, help tumbling down the hill a great deal faster than they had come up, but, as quick as thought, a man jumped down from the top of the diligence and put a stone under each wheel and stopped it. I had made up my mind before starting that it was of no use being frightened, so I took this incident as quite an ordinary occurrence, and was quite astonished afterwards to find that we had really been in danger. Henry wished us to get out, but the mayoral would not hear of it, and at last, after a great deal of shouting and cracking of the whip, the poor horses once more started and galloped up to the top of the hill, where we found a team of ten mules waiting for us. After this, the chief beauty of the road began. As we ascended the mountain the view on each side was bewilderingly beautiful, and the effects of light and shade glorious. The Pyrenees are covered with verdure, the grass looked to me greener even than in Ireland, and the road runs through the loveliest little glades and over tumbling brooks. Sometimes we passed under avenues of oaks and chestnuts, with a bright green sward beneath; sometimes through a waving sea of bracken fern. The road, of course, makes a zigzag up the mountain, so that you have always a precipice on one side. Up and down the rocks are numbers of merino sheep, with their long, wavy, silky hair, as white as driven snow. The cottages are very picturesque, and the people are simple and good-looking. As we passed through the villages, the men were all playing at ball or skittles, the priest, with his long gown tucked up round his waist, helping them. They all came to see the diligence go by, shouting and throwing up their caps.

We had a glorious sunset while we were still ascending. I feel as if I had never seen a sunset before that one; all others fade away before the memory of it. Some of the mountain peaks were shrouded in white clouds, which, as the sun sank, took a delicate rose tint; beneath us we had a rich valley, dotted with little white villages clustering round their church spires, and behind us, the long slope, down to the plain where Bayonne nestled among the chestnuts, at the mouth of the Adour. Here and there little spots were picked out in bright, glowing sunshine, while the rest of the landscape would be in sombre shadow. Sometimes, as we wound round the hill, we were ourselves in shade while one broad stream of glorious sunlight flooded the valley below, touching here and there upon the distant hilltops, and making Bayonne, with the glancing sea behind it, look like fairy land.

Then, when the sun finally disappeared behind the grey mountains, he left the west all one glow of rosy light, paling off into a greenish-pearl towards the east, and the clouds lying high up in the sky became golden and crimson, with soft snowy tips, while the mountains, behind which the sun had gone down, grew deep purple, fading off to a clear, cold grey. It became rapidly dark while we were watching the changing sky, and as we suddenly turned a sharp corner round the edge of the hill, we saw the full-moon rising from behind a distant peak, stately and still, and shedding a mellow light over the nearer hilltops. As the night advanced, this became stronger, and the scenery looked perfectly bewitching in the silvery light as we drove along, always at full gallop, with all the windows open, for it was balmy as a midsummer night. A light had been placed in the diligence high above our heads, which threw its gleam along the string of mules, and gave a most picturesque effect. Every now and then, when they seemed inclined to relax their efforts, a man, whose special duty it seemed to be, jumped down, and running by the side of the mules, whipped them up into a gallop, and then, catching the diligence as it passed, climbed like a monkey into his lofty perch, from whence he never ceased talking to his animals, calling to each by name, and sometimes breaking into snatches of a song, which was not in the least like the muleteer's song in the 'Rose of Castile,' but which harmonized well with the strangeness of the scene. As we dashed through the villages, the people stood at their doors and shouted as we passed. We changed mules about every hour and a half. Sometimes as we approached some lonely part of the road, where no house was visible, two or three wild, mysterious-looking men would rush suddenly across the way and stand in front of the approaching vehicle, throwing up their arms and shouting as if they meant to make us "stand and deliver;" and so in fact they did, but only our tired team of mules, and take a fresh one in its place. The men up in these mountains seem to have such an overwhelming amount of animal spirits, that they are perpetually venting them in leaping and shouting.

WE ENTER SPAIN.

We had passed the Spanish frontier before the sun set, crossing a bridge over a little stream, with a French guard-house on one side and a Spanish one on the other. We seemed to notice the difference immediately; the people on the Spanish side being so much more slovenly. We stopped at Elizondo, the first Spanish town we came to, about nine o'clock, to have the luggage examined. It was all unpacked—a work of some time—and carried into a large, empty room to be searched. The villagers had turned out to see us, and we walked between two lines of them as if we had been kings and queens at least. We got off very well; our portmanteaux being scarcely looked at. We walked about in the moonlight while the diligence was being repacked, and thought of you all at home. We arrived at Pampeluna at two o'clock A.M., and had to wait an hour in the most dismal of empty waiting-rooms in the station, where we got some flabby toast, spread apparently with tallow, and something that was called coffee, in cups half an inch thick. We had the railway-carriage to ourselves on starting again, and as we found it now very cold, we wrapped ourselves in our rugs and went to sleep. I awoke in time to see the dawn break and the sun rise, but it was over a flat, deserted-looking landscape. We breakfasted at Calatayud, and then started again for Madrid, where we arrived at five o'clock P.M., as you may imagine, rather tired.

Of the journey through Castile, I need say but a few words. I do not know where I got my idea of Spain, but I had an idea that it was to be something wonderful, of which the drive across the Pyrenees was merely a foretaste. Certainly, no one ever told me it was like one huge, dusty plain, with never a vestige of a tree or green leaf to be seen, and yet that is the truth. This land of romance and beauty lay stretching away on each side of us, a great, drab desert. In one place the scenery was fine in its way; rugged, barren-looking rocks and deep gorges, but generally it was the same eternally uniform dust-yard. And the people, too, looked more like savages than anything else; as dark as Indians, with their heads tightly bound up in a dirty red handkerchief, and no hair to be seen;

their clothes a mere mass of dust-coloured rags; in fact, face and dress were so completely a match for the surrounding dust that you really could only see there were people there by the shadow they cast in the blazing sunlight. The villages were mere clusters of mud-hovels the colour of the ground, with square holes for windows, innocent of glass, but with wooden shutters for winter or night use. At one of these villages, where are some celebrated baths, I was told the King was now staying, but I looked in vain for one hovel fitter than another to have the honour of lodging his Majesty. "Is this sunny, beautiful Spain?" I thought; sunny enough, Heaven knows! but the beauty had not come in our way yet. I was thankful when we came near Madrid, for the dust and heat had been terrible. We were obliged to keep the windows closed, and were nearly stifled. I had to tie my handkerchief over my mouth, like a respirator, to be able to breathe at all, for the carriage was full of dust.

As we came close to the station at Madrid, Henry pointed quite affectionately to some stumpy, dusty shrubs on a hill at a little distance, saying, "There is the Retiro, where you see the trees." My heart sank; were those the beautiful gardens of the Retiro one hears and reads of, or had we landed in some huge dust-bin? No doubt my first impressions were influenced by the fatigue and discomfort of the journey, but the utter absence of trees or hedgerows must always look wretched to an English person, especially if they are as ignorant as I was of the true state of the case.

We were met by quite a party of friends at the station, so I scarcely felt as if I were going to a strange place. This morning I had a walk with Henry, before breakfast, in the Retiro, which improves very much on a closer acquaintance.

The trees are very small and rather dusty, and the whole place is very formal in its arrangement, but the air is so delicious; a desert would be charming in such a climate.

Henry has a very nice side-saddle for me, and to-morrow one of the horses is to be tried with a horsecloth. We shall ride before breakfast, as it is still too hot at any other time in the day.

LETTER III.

Madrid, *September* 28.

I scarcely know how to give you a description of Madrid, for there is very little to say about it. It certainly is not a handsome city, and it strikes one as being ludicrously small.

It is a very marvellous thing to me how Spaniards can go on boasting as they do, that it is the "Capital of the World," for some of them at least must have seen other cities, and certainly any third-rate town in France or England would put Madrid to the blush, if, indeed, anything Spanish is capable of blushing. The only fine building is the Palace, which is beautifully situated on the edge of a steep cliff, at the foot of which runs the Manzanares, now a mere thread of sluggish water, winding along a broad bed of sand which shows how wide the river has been in flood times. The western windows command a view of what ought to be a beautiful stretch of land to the Guadarrama mountains, which bound one side of the horizon, but now, as there has been no rain since last April, everything is parched and dreary-looking. There are no hedges, the fields being divided from each other by mere trenches a few inches deep, and the high-roads, which are slightly raised above the surrounding ground, look wofully straight and uninteresting. From this spot, however, are to be seen the only trees which Madrid boasts outside the walls; for you look down to the right on a large park belonging to the Queen, called the Casa de Campo, which lies on the opposite side of the river and runs for some distance northward. On the slope below the Palace, and between it and the river, are the Royal gardens; nothing very extraordinary apparently, and kept, as all the gardens are here, in miserable disorder. The Palace was originally intended to be three times the size it is, as you see from the model which is kept in the museum of what it should have been; only one wing has been finished, but, as I said before, it is a handsome building. What strikes you most, however, is the slovenly, unfinished look of everything; the great courtyard, into which the principal door of the Palace opens, is worse paved than any stableyard in a dilapidated house in England, and the heaps of rubbish, where the building has ceased, still lie in full view of her Majesty's windows. There is a meagre little public garden at the back of the Palace, and joining on to the building itself is a row of miserable, tumble-down hovels following out the line of the cliff. The streets are all wretchedly paved, but they say it is owing to the extreme dryness and sandiness of the soil, which prevents any pavement remaining long in good order. The Puerta del Sol, of which the Madrileños boast so much, is a large open place in the centre of the town, with an immense fountain which is always playing. All the principal streets meet here, and the broad pavements are filled all day, and almost all night, by a crowd of idlers. The greatest part of one side of this square is taken up by the Government offices and the Post-Office; they are mill-like-looking places, which have once been stuccoed, but the plaster has peeled off in great patches, so that they look like the face of an old doll that has seen much service in a house where brothers abound. The lower part of the walls are covered with advertisements, so that these buildings are by no means ornamental, however useful they may be.

The streets are narrow, and are always crowded. In some of them there are respectable shops enough, but in many more they are mere open stalls. As far as width goes, the Calle Alcalá is the finest, running from the Puerta del Sol to the Prado. This Prado is the handsomest thing in Madrid, extending the whole length of the city and even much beyond it. It lies north and south, beyond the streets, but within the Alcalá gate—a handsome arch built by Charles III. At the south end of it there used to be the Atocha gate, but this has been removed, and the name only remains. There are broad walks for foot-passengers, well shaded by trees, and a handsome carriage-road, with fountains at intervals. To the upper end of the Prado, called the Fuente Castellano, all the fashionables resort in the evening when they are in town, but just now they are all at San Sebastian or Biarritz, and "La Corte" is supposed to be empty. The Retiro lies on a rising ground on the east side of the Prado, and the "Museo"—a long rambling building erected by Ferdinand VII. for the reception of the pictures when they were removed from the Escurial—stands between the two. The principal or south door of the Museum, which, however, never seems to be used, faces the Botanical Gardens, which occupy the remainder of the narrow strip, extending to the Atocha gate. They appear to combine the cultivation of zoology as well as botany, for there are a number of pens containing some sad-looking llamas, porcupines, cocks and hens, and other rare animals.

October 8.

I must confess that everything I have yet seen here, with the exception of the pictures, gives a wonderful idea of shabbiness and tawdriness. The Carrera San Geronimo is, perhaps, the principal street in Madrid, running parallel to the Alcalá from the Prado to the Puerta del Sol: it is a fine wide street at the lower end, with trees on each side, and the "Congreso de los Deputados" stands on the right as you go up towards the town. It is not, however, a very imposing building, with two dilapidated plaster lions sitting at the door, bearing unmistakable marks of past "pronunciamientos." These are, however, only keeping the places for marble lions who are coming by-and-by. Inside the Cortes, too, I saw nothing much to be admired, except some very beautiful pieces of marble which form the pedestals for the statues of Isabel la Católica and her husband. A great portion of the other side of the street is occupied by the house of the Duke de Medina Celi; and anything more tawdry and wretched in the way of building you cannot imagine. It reminds one of the houses that children build of coloured German bricks, and, like them, it has no depth. It has a great frontage to the street, but looked at endwise from the Prado it

BULLOCK DRIVER.

is only the width of two rooms, and looks like a thick wall with windows in. Even the front is only stuccoed, and the ornaments over the windows and doors are painted on the walls. This is, however, the case in most of the houses, except the very old ones, which have carved stone ornaments: but they are few and far between. Every building is coloured almost white, and is painfully dazzling in the blazing sun. The streets always look gay and lively, for they are always crowded and there is great variety of costume. Everything has a very foreign look to untravelled me: the clumsily-built carts, with their long string of six or eight mules straggling all across the road and jingling their bells; the heavy bullock-carts creeping along, with their driver, if you can call him so, walking before his beasts with a long stick over his shoulder to show them the way; the itinerant sellers of bread, melons, grapes, etc., each with his mule-load of wares, (for everything is carried in a kind of large pannier, an exaggerated carpenter's tool-basket), filling the air with discordant cries; the women with their light veils, and the men with their cumbrous cloaks, with here and there a bull-fighter, distinguishable by his little pigtail of plaited hair; and the fishmongers, who wear a peculiar dress,—I believe that of the Asturian peasantry,—all make up a curious scene. You see also a great number of

ASTURIAN NURSES.

Asturian nurses in their national dress. It is not the custom, it seems, here for ladies to bring up their own children, and the wet nurses all come from Asturias. They are dressed by their mistresses, who seem to vie with each other in turning

ASTURIAN NURSE—IN NATIONAL COSTUME.

out their servants as richly as possible. The costume is very pretty. A short skirt of silk, or sometimes even velvet, generally scarlet or very bright blue, with a bodice open in front and laced across. An apron of black and silver, or black and gold, tied behind with a bow and long ends; a coloured silk handkerchief over the head, from under which the hair hangs in two long plaits below the waist. The skirt of the dress is generally trimmed with broad bands of velvet, sometimes edged with gold or silver, and the body, which is cut square about the throat, with innumerable little silver buttons. They wear long earrings, and a chain of silver or coral, coiled many times round their neck.

At almost every second step you meet a priest in

PRIEST, WITH HIS GIMLET HAT.

his long black cloak and "gimlet" hat; so called, because the broad brim is rolled over the crown from the sides, and looks very much like the handle of a gimlet. They are exceedingly coarse-looking and ill-favoured men, and seem to be of the lowest of the people. Occasionally you will see a picador riding down to the bull-ring—if there is going to be a performance there—on his miserable skeleton of a horse; his legs padded to an immense size, and looking most quaint in his wide-brimmed, yellow hat and jacket of gold tissue.

Tell sisters that while they are just thinking of turning out of bed in a morning, Henry and I are galloping across country, with a glorious blue sky overhead; but do not ask what under our feet. I told you already that the country all round Madrid is absolutely hideous at this time of the year; a mere dingy wilderness of dust; so you must not imagine us riding through pleasant lanes or green fields. Nevertheless we manage to enjoy ourselves, and, indeed, there is something to admire in the very barrenness of the scenery; for one thing you have the view of the whole horizon, just as you have at sea, with the Guadarramas bounding one side of it. The light and shade on these mountains is always beautiful, and then the climate is so delicious that you can forgive a great deal. Yesterday we were out a long time, for we discovered a road with some living trees on it, and, moreover, coming to a great common, we dashed off the road and had a good gallop, jumping the horses over all the ditches we could find; which, however, I am bound to say was not very many, nor were they very wide.

On Monday night we went to the opera, and heard Mario and Borghi Mamo in the 'Barber of Seville.' Henry has taken a stall for the season, and he and a friend, who has the next seat, take it in turns to use both, so that we go very often. It is a capital house, about the same size as Covent Garden; the whole of the lower part is filled with comfortable stalls, and there is only a small gallery at the top for the "gods." Ladies do not dress, except in the boxes. Between the acts there is a long interval, that would drive a London audience wild, during which the gentlemen go about paying visits to their acquaintances. You can obtain admittance to the theatre by paying a peseta (tenpence), and if you have friends in the boxes, can join them, so that once inside you can go to any part of the house where you can obtain a seat. Many of the gentlemen also go and smoke in the passages, and as the doors are all open, the place becomes filled with smoke in a very short time. There are some cigars here which are called "entre-actos," just large enough to last during this interval. The instrumental music and scenery were not very brilliant, and the minor parts of the opera were filled by wretched singers.

On Tuesday we went to see Léotard. He performs in a large circus; a permanent building, which is fitted up like a theatre, with private boxes and stalls all round. Here the ladies were all in full dress. Our box was next to the one where Léotard's perch was fixed, so we had a capital view. I was very much pleased with the performance; it is so graceful, and gives you no feeling of danger. I liked, too, to watch him take the spring and alight again on his perch.

I am afraid I shall not learn Spanish quickly, for my little English maid speaks it perfectly, and she interprets for me, so I am not compelled to make the effort.

I do not think Spaniards need talk so much of our changeable climate, for yesterday was so hot that we had to creep along in the shade, and to-day there is a howling wind, and cold, drizzling rain. After being out walking this morning, I came in with my hands quite benumbed.

PRIEST, WITH HIS GIMLET HAT.

LETTER IV.

MADRID, *October* 18, 1863.

ANOTHER howling, miserable day; but I do not care if it rains cats and dogs, for I have a bright fire in the most luxurious of libraries, and the moans of the wind outside only make a pleasant contrast to the comfort within. But the real secret of my content is, that I have just been relieved from the horrors of having to spend a whole week alone in this heathen country, eating my meals in pompous silence in the presence of two mute men-servants, and passing my days like a prisoner in solitary confinement. Henry and Mr. Smith were to have started this evening to meet the English party at Benevente, but a telegraphic message has just arrived, to our great delight, saying they are coming straight on to Madrid. I dare say I should have managed to get over the time in some way; some of our friends would have come in to chat with me; but I am not sorry to escape the ordeal just now while I am quite fresh to the place and its ways; for I must confess to feeling a little dreadful sometimes in the midst of people jabbering an utterly unknown tongue, and being perfectly unable to make myself understood without help. I hear Jane singing away over her work, and it is quite pleasant to hear her sweet English voice, for the Spaniards seem to me to be a singularly unmusical people, and while the men's voices are something between a grunt and a growl, those of the women sound like the clatter of pans and dishes. The servants and people in the streets are constantly singing, but it is a most inharmonious performance, beginning, generally, on a high note, and wavering irregularly down the scale; or a monotonous fandango, which is like nothing earthly, and is so far removed from a tune that you wonder how two people ever manage to hit upon the same notes twice together. The lower class of peasantry have very bad countenances; they are very much like the extremely low Irish both in face and manner. They seem quite a separate class from the domestic servants, who look honest enough. It is very strange to see men doing what our female servants do at home,—sweeping, dusting, and housemaiding generally. In the hotels they have no women servants at all.

October 30.

Our English friends arrived on Saturday night, looking very dusty and tired. They were in capital spirits, however, and seem to have enjoyed their journey. Yesterday morning (Sunday) they appeared here about eleven o'clock, and after paying a visit to the stables,—which, by the way, are under the house, in what would be the cellar in England, —we all went to the Museum, where we spent a couple of hours most pleasantly. It is, I believe, almost, if not quite, the finest collection of pictures in the world. The Spanish school is, of course, largely represented,—especially Velasquez,—and the Dutch too; but I never could care for Dutch pictures. There are some beautiful Raphaels, and two or three Claudes, which are exquisite. There is a 'Holy Family' by the former, which once belonged to England, and which I believe was sold in the time of the Commonwealth. One can hardly forgive Cromwell if this is true. It is very beautiful; the face of the Virgin is so child-like, and yet so lovely, crowned by a coronet of golden hair. We are so near to the gallery that we go very often, and spend an hour or two there, as foreigners are always admitted. Just now they are altering the principal gallery, and putting down a new floor, so that many of the pictures are unhung, or placed in some of the smaller rooms until the other is finished.

Afterwards we had a long walk in the Retiro, and had only just time to dress and go off to the "Inglaterra" to dine with our English friends. We had a most amusing evening. When Henry and I went in, we found the three Englishmen vainly attempting to explain something to Señor Martinez, who had also been invited to dinner, and who, much to the consternation of his hosts, had arrived a little early. Neither party being able to speak anything but their own language, the conversation had been carried on under great difficulties.

They had, however, managed to inform the Spaniard that they had been writing to their wives by pointing to the letters, and saying "Esposa mia:" but we were greeted with great joy, and a universal peal of laughter as both sides began relating their efforts towards understanding each other.

At dinner Mr. Wilson was quite distressed at seeing the unfortunate Spaniard unable to speak or comprehend what was being said, except when Henry translated for him; and having been told that Spanish was very like Latin, conceived the brilliant idea that by using only such English words as were derived from Latin he might make himself understood.

The language he succeeded in concocting, was singular, to say the least, and was highly amusing to his listeners. After great labour and infinite pains to avoid all Saxon words, he made up the

following sentence, which came out in jerks:—
"In Inglaterra we (pointing to the company, to express Englishmen generally) imbibe a grand quantity de Xeres" (pointing to the sherry bottle).

We were not surprised to hear the next day that Señor Martinez thought the stout Englishman was a little mad. It was curious, however, to find how entirely the language of conversation with us is Saxon, a fact which you notice when you are making an effort to use words of Latin derivation only.

In the midst of dinner we were told we were sitting in one of the rooms of the old Inquisition. It was impossible to help a shudder as one looked round and thought of the awful scenes that might have taken place there; but I believe the present building was erected, after the worst times of the Inquisition, on the site of the old one: the cellars and dungeons are the same. It is a queer, rambling place, full of long passages, but there is nothing very wonderful about it now. Don José, the proprietor, is a collector of curiosities, and the rooms seem all filled with extraordinary pictures and cases of old china.

There is nothing I have been so much disappointed in as the Spanish cloak, about the grace of which we hear so much in England. They might be graceful if they were simple cloaks, but they have a great cape to them which hangs off the shoulders

MANNER OF WEARING THE "CAPA."

like a policeman's waterproof, and cuts the figure in two in the most ungraceful way; and then they have a narrow lining of velvet or silk, generally of some gaudy, flaring colour, which is carefully disposed outside for show in flinging it over the shoulder. I do not see anything graceful in them, and they are horribly effeminate. They are, however, going out of fashion among the upper classes, and you only see them on second-rate people.

The Mantilla, too, is dying out, and is only to be seen on some old ladies. I cannot imagine how it

OLD LADY WEARING THE MANTILLA.

can ever have been pretty, for it consists of a breadth of heavy, watered silk about three yards long, with a fall of deep lace sewn at the edge, and is fastened into the hair at the back and under the chin, the ends falling over the shoulders in front, so that from behind it makes the wearer look like an extinguisher. The lace is intended to come over the head and face like a veil, but it is generally allowed to fall over the silk behind. But the light 'velas,' which the younger ladies wear, are very pretty;

THE "MODERN VELA."

they are either made of a light French lace or mere black-spotted tulle, and are worn in the same way as a mantilla, but being transparent, they are very.

graceful and becoming. French bonnets are, however, rapidly driving out even the velas, and it is a great pity, for they do not suit the Spanish face. The old custom of wearing black is also passing away, and you see the Madrileñas on the Prado, gorgeous in red and green, like parrots. They display a singular want of taste in their assortment of colours; indeed, they generally appear to have tried how many different ones they can put on at once. A blue dress and a violet mantle, a green bonnet and pink gloves, is not an uncommon mixture. At church it is still considered the thing to appear in black, but it is by no means universally done, as I have seen very brilliant plumages going into Mass; but bonnets are never worn in church. Numbers of Spanish women become quite bald when they grow old, and as they never wear caps, but go about with nothing but a thin veil over their heads,—and sometimes not even that,—they do not look very beautiful. Henry declares that they pull their hair all out by the roots in dressing them over the immense horns which are fashionable now; and certainly some of them do look as if they could not shut their eyes.

To-day the English party have gone off to Guadalaxara, but they dine with us this evening, and afterwards we are going to one of the theatres. They are very much disappointed at not being able to see a bull-fight; but the weather is so cold and rainy that none will take place at present: and, indeed, I believe the season is almost over for regular bull-fights. In the winter they have only what they call "Corridas de Novillos;" that is, of young bulls which are brought up to try. They are, of course, not allowed to be killed or injured, though there are generally two bulls "de muerto," as a kind of treat at the last. If they are brave, and show fight well, they are taken back to their pasture and kept until they are six or eight years old: the cowardly bulls are used as draught oxen. In these mock fights any one is allowed to enter the arena; but as the bulls have knobs on the end of their horns, they cannot do very great damage. I believe there are sometimes very amusing scenes, but the *habitués* of the bull-ring turn up their noses at "corridas de novillos." I have been asked very often to go, and a friend of ours has offered me his private box, and says I could come out if I found it at all unpleasant; but from all I hear of the spectacle—at least of a regular bull-fight—I do not think it would be likely to gratify me; though English ladies do go, and, to the surprise of the gentlemen, sit out the whole performance. In England we are accustomed to hear people talking very virtuously of the barbarity of this amusement, and its brutalizing effect on the mind, but I must confess that my countrymen here seem almost as fond of a bull-fight as the Spaniards themselves, and are by no means irregular attendants. They all agree, at first, that it is a cruel and disgusting sight, but whether "*ce n'est que le premier pas qui coûte,*" or that the agility and bravery of the toreros overbalance the unpleasant part of the performance, certain it is that many of them thoroughly enjoy a bull-fight, and miss few good ones.

We have not had a ride for two days, for the weather has been very disagreeable. It is, I fancy, colder now than in England, as the Guaderramas are crested with snow, and the wind from that quarter is very piercing. One feels it the more, too, because the change from hot, sultry weather was so marvellously sudden. We keep large fires, but in this country everything seems to be out of order; the windows won't fasten, and the doors won't shut, and you can put your fingers through the chinks in the woodwork. It is only in new houses that fireplaces are to be found at all, and then they are of the most primitive description; the Spaniards are accustomed to use large pans of charcoal, called *braseros*, which are wretched contrivances for warming you, and excellent ones for giving you a headache and half stifling you. The houses are all built in flats, which is one reason why Madrid occupies so small a space in comparison to its population. The system has its advantages, for you get much better and more lofty rooms than you would in a small house: but, on the other hand, in a house of your own you can only have two next-door neighbours, while in a flat it is possible to have four— and suppose they are all musical! The new houses are very airy and handsome, but the old ones seem all passages and dark rooms; they are built in the form of a quadrangle, enclosing a paved court called a *patio*. One flat frequently runs round all the sides of this yard, so that many of the rooms have no light except that which comes from the passage, and the servants are generally packed away in perfectly dark dens, with no attempt at ventilation of any kind. The lower windows, when they look into the street, are protected by a projecting sort of iron cage; this is called the *rega*, and it is where most of the lovemaking is done. To talk with a lover through the rega is called *pelando el pavo* (plucking the turkey), but I cannot find out why. We have several affectionate couples in our street, who carry on their little affairs from the balcony; that is to say, the lady stands in her balcony while her lover remains on the pavement below, and they screech to each other, apparently not at all disturbed by the publicity of their conversation, or by the fact that there is a couple on each side engaged in the same way. I saw a young lady carefully lowering a little parcel, or letter, to her admirer the other evening, but as it passed the balcony below, from which another young lady was entertaining her friend, it was very quietly caught, and having been taken to the window for a few moments, was allowed to continue its downward journey; though how the three men waiting on the pavement below knew from which of their respective goddesses it came, I do not know.

October 8.

A brilliant idea has just struck me! I will send a huge letter home by Willie, so that I can write whenever I feel inclined, and you need not read it all at once, but can take it in homœopathic doses. I find writing the best possible remedy for loneliness, and though my letters are sometimes never posted, but come to an untimely end, they have fulfilled their mission in being written, and can go to their grave with an easy conscience. I have scarcely read at all since I came here, except the 'Westminster Review' and 'Fraser,' for I have never felt really settled yet, but I mean to be very diligent, for as I am alone for seven or eight hours every day, I ought to make good use of my time. Hitherto, I have kept continually changing my occupation;—practising for an hour, then studying

Spanish for a time, reading, working, etc.; for I am fully determined not to be dull, and can manage to make the time pass very quickly; but I look forward with such pleasure to the hour for our ride. We are going to spend Sunday at Toledo one of these days. I believe it is one of the most interesting places in Spain. Whenever I hear any one speaking of any place being pretty, I always ask, "Are there any trees?" The answer is invariably, "No." But in the south, I am told, the country is really beautiful.

Spaniards live on and in the sun. I believe if there were none for a month, the whole nation would be found dead. The streets are full all day long of people, *tomando el sol*, literally "taking the sun" and "propping up the corners," as they say here. Even the shopkeepers in some of the small streets bring out their three-legged stools and sit in the gutter in front of their shops, scarcely troubling themselves to get up when a customer appears. They always ask double what they mean to take, and are accustomed to the Spaniards haggling with them over every pound of grapes, and probably leaving the shop two or three times before they buy anything.

Some of the mules that come in from the country look very picturesque, with a network of crimson silk tassels over their heads, and a bright-coloured *manta* thrown across their sleek, glossy backs. These mantas serve many purposes; they are made of two breadths, of a silk and woollen mixture, in broad stripes of several brilliant colours, sewn together, with a piece left open at one side, like a purse. Sometimes they are thrown across the mule and serve as saddle-bags, sometimes they do duty as a wrap for the master. All the horses, mules, and oxen have bells round their collars, the latter generally have one large bell, which hangs underneath the head. It is so curious to see the use that is made of these tame oxen in driving in the wild bulls. Twice over, when we have been riding, we have met them coming in for the Corrida on the following day. The oxen go first, clanging their bells, and the bulls follow them, generally quite quietly. If a bull is so fierce that he cannot be killed, and it is necessary to take him out of the

E

arena, two of these oxen are driven in; they place themselves one on each side of the poor tortured brute, and he walks out between them in the most amiable manner. They are also sent out to bring back the bulls if they escape from their pasture, or, as often happens, from the arena in the villages, where the bull-fights are held in the plaza, which is only temporarily barricaded. Once, however, we met the drove of bulls coming into Madrid, and they had passed the ring and gone down the lane where we were, before the picadores who were driving them could get them turned—I do not know if the oxen were with them or not; we saw some people in front of us, at a little distance, gesticulating wildly and making signs to us, which we could not understand, until suddenly the whole drove came tearing round a corner quite close to us. I jumped my horse over a copse and ditch which bounded the road and galloped off across a field where a young crop of some sort was coming up, and when I looked back at what I considered a safe distance, I saw a bull standing on the very spot on the bank which I had jumped; however, they were driven off and I rode back to look for Henry. He had put his horse at the ditch, too, but he swerved and bolted with him in another direction. That is the nearest approach to a bull-fight I am likely to see, so I must make the most of it.

We have glorious weather again after two days' dismal, howling wind and rain, but the air is keen and autumn-like, and the hot days have taken their final departure.

October 14.

My days of unlimited writing are coming to an end, for William talks of leaving for Valencia tomorrow or Thursday, and so home, by way of Barcelona and Perpignan. We all went to the Zarzuela Theatre last night, and, though I could not understand much of the Spanish, by help of Henry's interpretation I enjoyed it very much. The piece was called, 'The Horns of the Bull,' and was very amusing. A whole *cuadrilla*, as it is called, or band of bull-fighters, appeared on the stage in their costumes, which are most gorgeous—generally crimson or blue silk or velvet, almost covered with gold.

The fun of the piece turns on an old gentleman who has laid a wager that he will kill a bull in the arena, and then in great alarm sends for a celebrated espada to give him lessons, which he does, using a chair to represent the bull. In most of the other theatres I have seen here I have found the pieces awfully dull and stereotyped; there appears, indeed, to be nothing to act. The idea of scenery seems to be an octagon room with a door in each division, and a table and two chairs in the middle. A woman enters by one of the doors and stands by the table; a man rushes in with his hat and stick in his hand and talks to her without ceasing for half an hour; then they both go out by different doors, and presently she reappears through another door, and then a fresh character appears through another, and there is another half-hour's conversation; and then the first one comes back, and so on, and so on, until all the doors have been used and all the characters in the piece have stood by the table and talked, and then the curtain drops, and that is all. But the 'Astas del Toro' is really good and quite intelligible, even with such an imperfect knowledge of Spanish as mine necessarily is, and there are some pretty songs introduced into it. I am afraid I shall never learn Spanish, I have so little opportunity, or rather necessity, for speaking it. I study the grammar very diligently, but I find it rather dull work.

Already the sun has played us false again, and we have had drip, drip, drip, all day long. In spite of the miserable day, the English party have gone off to Toledo to see the lions there. They came for me this morning, but I did not feel inclined to be drenched, as I shall have other opportunities of seeing the place.

October 15.

The Inglaterra party leave this evening, and Henry goes with them as far as Valencia, so that I shall be alone for two or three days. I have sent the photographs and a whole budget of letters by Willie. I am afraid you will find the latter very dull, but you must remember that I wrote them whenever I felt particularly lonely, by way of passing the time. I do not attempt to tell you anything that you will find much better told in Ford, but merely the impression Madrid makes on me, and those things which are most unlike what we are accustomed to at home.

Henry talked of my going with the party to Valencia; but I thought I should enjoy going by ourselves by-and-by, and so preferred remaining behind, though I shall find it dull enough, I dare say. The thing I find most tiresome is, that I cannot stir an inch out of doors by myself, as it is not proper to do so here. I believe married ladies may go out alone, but you never see them do so; if they have not a friend with them, they take a servant; and if I only want to go across the street, I must have a nurse to take care of me, which effectually prevents my going out at all; so that when Henry is away, I should never leave the house if some of my friends did not kindly come and take me out.

We have been leading a very dissipated life while Willie and his friends have been here,—going to the theatre or opera almost every night, and seeing all the lions of Madrid. These, it must be confessed, however, are not very numerous. After the picture gallery the next best sight is the armoury, which, though small, is a very interesting collection, and is beautifully arranged. It is in one of the dilapidated, cow-house-looking places which join on to the Queen's palace; but the room is good enough when you are in it. There is the sword of the Cid, and a number of suits of armour belonging to Charles V. and Philip II.,—"Rey de Inglaterra," as they always take care to call him; also of Cardinal Ximenes, Columbus, Cortés, and Pizarro; and a wonderful old leather sedan-chair, in which Charles V. used to be carried to battle when he had gout. There is also the helmet of Francis I., taken when he was made prisoner; his sword was given up again to the French a short time ago, and now they have only a copy of it; the helmet of Boabdil el Chico, the last of the Moors, and a quantity of arms, dresses, ornaments, etc., taken from Peru and Mexico.

In the old Plaza de la Villa they show you the tower in which Francis I. was confined while a prisoner in Madrid. There is literally nothing else to be seen in this "capital of the world" but the

Museo, the armoury, and two very celebrated pictures of Murillo in the Academia; therefore, to professional sight-seers it must prove a very dull place; and, indeed, I have heard of several English travelling parties who have been so disgusted at it that they have left the day after their arrival.

Thursday, October 22.

Henry being at the opera, I am sitting "my lone," as the Irish say, though I have not been so long. Mr. Smith and Charlie dined with us, and have only just left, as I have been entertaining them in a very delightful manner. We live here in an utter disregard of the forms and ceremonies of civilized life,—every one coming in and going out, and doing generally what seemeth good in his own eyes; but as there is no Mrs. Grundy to keep us in order, it is of no consequence. We are never alone. This morning, for the first time since my arrival in Madrid, we breakfasted by ourselves. We take a cup of coffee and a piece of French roll in the morning before going out, and have *déjeuner à la fourchette* at twelve, and dinner at seven. I like this division of the day very much. This morning we had a long ride, and a splendid view of the mountains. You would scarcely fancy our enjoying our rides if you saw the country we go over. I remember reading in some book of the beautiful walks and drives about Madrid which Charles III. laid out; but I must say, that though we explore in every direction, we have never fallen in with any of them. The *caminos reales* (high-roads) are very generally good and well kept; but, besides them, there is nothing in the shape of a road to be seen. A track is made through the fields by one mule-cart and followed by others, until it becomes a regular path, but no attempt is ever made to do anything with it. In dry weather these tracks are five or six inches deep in dust, and in wet weather they are impassable for mud. The carts go in up to the axles in the holes, and when these become very bad, a few old broken pots are thrown in to fill them up; but when they are past all mending, the simple remedy is to make a little *détour* round the hole, irrespective of the feelings of the fields on each side.

We do not, however, trouble the roads much, but go right across country; for, as there are no hedges, there is nothing to stop us; occasionally we come to a little ditch, two or three feet wide, but we can scarcely ever find anything in the shape of a jump. We frequently make use of the dry beds of the little rivers which are very common here; they are capital for riding on, being smooth and sometimes firm, like sea-sands, but they are very often used as roads, and are then quite spoiled, until the next wet season levels them again. When a mule dies here it is skinned, and then left just where it dropped, apparently, by the roadside or in the field; we are always coming across them in our rambles, with two or three heavy vultures hovering near, which soon leave nothing but white bones. One place where we sometimes ride we have christened the valley of Jehosaphat, so full is it of these bleached bones. To add to the other delights of the country, outside of Madrid there are in different places large dust-heaps, where all the rubbish and offal of the city is daily carted out; for every one throws his refuse out of the windows or doors into the street, and early in the morning carts go round to collect it. The men who accompany these carts ring a bell as they go along, and call out in a melancholy tone, which reminds one of the "Bring forth your dead" of the Plague time. Troops of meagre, villainous-looking dogs roam about with them, fighting and snarling over the bones and scraps they may find, and, finally, follow the carts out to the dust-heaps, where they spend their day in company with droves of pigs, which are taken there to feed, and a crowd of wretched, half-starved human beings, rooting in the dirt for prey. We are beginning to know the position of these pig-lands, and give them a wide berth, for it is not pleasant to have them between the wind and your nose; but if we do chance to come upon one unexpectedly, the moment a horse appears down come the dogs in a troop, and you are likely to have a nice John Gilpin chase. The only thing you can do is to pull up and remain quite quiet, when the dogs bark round you in concert for a time, and then go off again to assist their human and porcine companions in wallowing in the mire; but if you go on at all quickly, they are back again in a moment; and when you hear that they are great brindled brutes, tall enough to snap at my foot in the stirrup, as they constantly do, you can imagine they are not pleasant company.

All this sounds delightful, does it not? But the mere fact of riding a good horse on a beautiful morning goes far to make you overlook many difficulties. I think we must be considered quite mad here, for the Spaniards never go beyond the one fashionable mile of the Fuente Castellano,—the ladies' mile of Madrid,—and their horses are taught to play all sorts of antics and foolish circus tricks. I must confess to having a supreme desire to see one of the Madrid *pollos* (which may be freely translated "puppies") pitched over his horse's head, for they ride them with a cruelly tight curb, and then drive their spurs in to make them curvet; and the horses do not seem to have spirit to resent it. It makes me so angry that I wish sometimes I could change myself into a horse for a time, and take one of these darlings out for his airing. And they have a seat, too, which would make them an easy prey, for they sit with their legs about half a yard from the horse's flank, and with their toes gracefully pointed inwards, except, of course, when they are spurring. The only advantage I can see in this mode of riding is, that if the horse suddenly came down under him, the rider would be comfortably placed in the position of the Colossus of Rhodes. A friend of ours compared the Fuente Castellano at the fashionable hour to a *chevaux de frise* on horseback; and certainly, if we ever do by chance pass through it, it is at imminent risk to my habit from the outsticking spurs, more especially as there is no law of the road, or if there is, no one dreams of obeying it, but they pass just as the fancy takes them, even in the most crowded places, while the carriages struggle all over the road, making a serpentine track in the dust, and the coachmen sit with their legs doubled up under the seat and the reins hanging loose over the horses' backs, while their whip dangles off at the side like a fishing-rod. Strangers are always astonished at the number of carriages in Madrid; but a Spaniard will keep a carriage when he can scarcely afford to keep himself, and two or three young "pollos" will club together to set up a phaeton, and will take it in turns to go and be driven about the ladies' mile in the evening.

The horses have the credit of being very fine I believe, and certainly a good Andaluz is very beautiful in its way, but I do not admire them. They have wonderfully thick necks, and, one and all, Roman noses, which make them look like Jews, and very long manes and tails, the latter frequently touching the ground. In wet weather, these are tied up into a huge bob, and look like those wedge-shaped tails which Noah's horses had, if we may believe the models of them which have come down to the present day in the children's arks.

They are so low in the shoulder that when mounted you feel perpetually as if you were sliding over your horse's head; and then their paces are so disagreeable. They canter in the true rocking-horse style, and cannot trot at all. The pace about which one hears so much looks very well with the mules, with whom it is apparently natural, and is the very thing for a long journey, as you have not to rise, and the animal gets over the ground very quickly, and without much fatigue. But the horses are regularly broken into it, and it completely spoils their trot. It gives them a most awkward look when you see them coming towards you, as they throw out their fore-legs with a sideway, shuffling movement.

I wish you could see the cab-horses. They are like no animal you ever saw, except in the drawings of children. They give me the idea of having been made in a large manufactory; the barrels being finished first and passed on to another department to supply legs; while a third hand sticks on the heads and tails as a finishing touch.

I believe we are going to Valencia next week, but we are not quite certain. To-night we go to the Opera to hear the sisters Marchisio in 'Norma.' I cannot say I admire these ladies much, though the younger one made a very good Azucena in 'Il Trovatore.'

I am becoming almost fond of Madrid. There are plenty of trees inside the walls, though they are small; they are watered twice a day, and look rather pretty with a little stream of clear water running from tree to tree and eddying round their trunks. Wherever the ground is irrigated it is wonderfully luxuriant, but it spoils the appearance of a garden, as it is obliged to be laid out so formally, on account of the water channels. The whole of the Retiro is irrigated, and in a most primitive way. You have seen those drawings of Indian wheels for raising water by means of little earthenware jars fastened to a long rope, which goes down into the

NORIA FOR RAISING WATER.

well and brings up a few drops in each jar; these Spanish *norias* are just the same, and one might have imagined they were originally set up by Jacob, so antiquated and rude do they appear. The pole by means of which the wheel is turned is a young tree left just as it was cut down, except that the branches are off, and a mule paces slowly round with it, while the string of jars come up, each with about a teacupful of water, which is emptied into a leaky wooden trough as they go down again, and from the trough into the irrigation channels; so the watering business is rather a long one, but that is of no consequence in this extremely leisurely country.

On the Prado there are plenty of seats under the trees, and the splash of the numerous fountains sounds very pleasant. On one broad walk the people congregate in the evening after sundown when it is warm, and remain till eleven or twelve o'clock, forming little open-air "tertulias," as friends meet together and form circles of chairs. Others walk up and down, or sit reading the evening newspapers under the gaslights; while water-carriers and fruit-sellers go about calling their wares, and street musicians, with their guitars and hurdy-gurdies, add to the general uproar. In the carriages the ladies dress very gaily, and have their hair elaborately dressed with flowers and coloured ribbons, and as the vela is merely a nominal covering, and is thrown back over the shoulders, their costume looks more fit for a ball than a drive. I am much disappointed in the Spanish women, of whose graceful walk and carriage we hear so much. In Madrid they are certainly about the worst walkers I ever saw, wearing awfully tight stays, and small boots with extremely high heels. The children are all bandy-legged, and I see no reason to suppose they grow straighter as they grow older; indeed, as the ladies waddle in a wonderful way, I think the evidence tends the other way; but as they never take up their dresses, but trail them half a yard behind them, raising a cloud of dust far above their heads, I have no means of verifying this hypothesis. Every one asks if the Spanish women are not very beautiful. They have almost all good eyes and eyebrows, but otherwise the Madrileñas are not very lovely as a rule. I do not give my own opinion, which might be considered invidious, but that of all the Englishmen whom I have met here.

In Andalusia, I believe, the women are very handsome.

October 29.

We have had the Empress of the French here, staying with Queen Isabel, and with her mother, the Countess of Montijo. I wonder how she felt coming back as Empress to her old home and among her old friends. There have been great festivities here in her honour, and an immense amount of driving about in gilt carriages. There was a grand bull-fight announced to take place, with all the most celebrated toreros, at which the Empress, who is said to be very fond of this amusement, was to be present; but at the last moment she drove off to see her mother at Carabanchel instead. Everybody was in amazement, and every one knew the exact reason of the sudden change,—only, unfortunately, no two people knew the same exact reason. One was that the Emperor had telegraphed at the last moment forbidding his wife to go: another, that it was on account of the Princess Anne Murat, who had come in attendance on the Empress, to the great annoyance of the Spaniards, some of whom seem inclined to look upon it as an insult; and wise heads foretold a "row" at the bull-fight if she appeared there. But *quien sabe?*

On Sunday afternoon we had a long ride, and explored the road along the riverside, which I told you in a former letter lies below the hill on which the Palace stands. We had quite a pleasant surprise; the road is almost like an English one, bordered with trees on each side—real trees! It follows the course of the river, and on the other side it is bounded by a property of the King's, called the Florida, which is prettily planted. When you come to the end of this, the road continues through an immense kind of park, with *bonâ fide* grass and clumps of trees in it: to be sure they are only small, but if you only knew what it is to see anything green in this desert! We had also a fine view of the mountains from a new point. We rode about all the afternoon under the trees, tearing along the dry bed of a river, or up the hills for the sake of a view from the top. We came home by moonlight—for here we have scarcely any twilight,

and almost immediately after the sun sets it becomes
dark, or moonlight, as the case may be—after a
three hours' ride, agreeing that if we had fresh
horses we would go back and do it all over again.
It really is not fair to Madrid that people should
pass through it without seeing it from this side, for
it is really rather pretty, and is so different from
the other parts of the country around; and yet I
fancy that few strangers ever do see it. On this
road is the village of El Pardillo, where Longfellow
quartered himself and which he describes in his
' Outre Mer.' He certainly showed his taste, as it
is the only pretty place in the neighbourhood. You
come upon a curious scene as you descend the steep
hill from the Palace to the river, for this same river
is the universal wash-tub of Madrid. For a great
distance up the stream the place seems alive with
washerwomen, kneeling on the bankside, and scrub-
bing the linen on a board which slopes down into
the water. The quantity of water is so small, except in the rainy season, that it is stopped, for the
accommodation of each laundress, by a little bank
or board jutting out into the stream. All the centre

of the river—now a broad sandbank—is a forest of clothes lines, with their miscellaneous ornaments.

As you may imagine, under these circumstances our clothes are not wont to be very beautifully washed here, and look as if a little hot water would be an advantage to them; while the rubbing they undergo on the boards soon brings them into holes.

I wish there were any way of preserving some of our beautiful weather here and sending it over to you; for, though not quite so warm as it was, it is bright and sunny, and the air is only just sharp enough to be very pleasant. The trees are beginning to change their colour, but the leaves have scarcely fallen at all yet.

We had one wet day this week, just enough to soften the roads; but certainly when it does rain here, there is no mistake about it; it comes straight down from morning to night without stopping a moment; and when at last it comes to an end, you must walk up the middle of the street if you do not wish to be drowned, for the pipes which carry the water off the roofs of the houses project some feet from the edge, and pour their whole torrent down on the heads of the innocent passer-by. I thought the top of our cab was coming in the other night on our way to the opera, as one after another of these waterspouts caught us, and splashed off again into the street.

Madrid is a curious mixture of extreme French fashions and semi-civilized ideas; of pomp and glory and squalor. The Spaniards pride themselves on the magnificence of their court. The Queen never goes out without a guard of soldiers, and at least six horses to her carriage, with an empty carriage of respect, also with six horses, behind; and her suite follow in the same style, while a perfect cavalcade of outriders in cocked hats—looking very much like Jack Sheppards—are in attendance; not to mention equerries, etc. etc. It takes six horses to cart the little Infante's perambulator up to the Retiro; and the child himself drives about with the same state as the Queen. As for the Empress, they drove her about in a glass coach with innumerable horses, all with coronets of crimson plumes on their heads, and a procession of outriders, soldiers, and state carriages, that extended almost as far as you could see down the Prado; and there sat the lady whom the Queen delighted to honour, in a simple mauve dress and a little black hat, looking very pretty and quiet in her gingerbread coach, with the poor little King sitting opposite her, almost smothered under his cocked hat and feathers. Then, again, whenever a royal carriage, whether it be empty or not, passes a barrack, the sentries have to blow a trumpet before it, and the guard turn out. And as Madrid is full of barracks and also full of royal carriages, always driving about some of the hundred and fifty Infantes, aunts and uncles, brothers and sisters, or cousins of their Majesties, the place is in a chronic state of trumpeting, and the guard pass their time for ever turning out and in again.

On the occasion of any grand procession, all the grandees' carriages appear with their six horses decorated with coloured plumes, and their servants equally fine. And yet it is quite an everyday sight to see the wash of the family hung out to dry over the drawing-room balcony, even in the handsomest houses; and out of the window of a duke's palace the other day, I saw a bright yellow flannel petticoat waving in the breeze. Imagine an assortment of shirts and other articles gracefully decorating the windows of Apsley House!

Yesterday evening Henry and I had a walk on the Prado to watch the sunset. I never saw a more beautiful sky; as the warm tints began to fade out, the first crescent of the moon hung like a delicate silver thread above the rosy-tipped clouds. I do not wonder at the southerns being proud of their sky; but grant it them, and give me dear little England, with her hedgerows and meadows, her sweet wild flowers and babbling streams, ay, and her cloudy days too, for life is not all sunshine.

November 6, 1863.

Mr. and Mrs. —— arrived last week, so I shall have, at least, one female companion. I do not know any Spanish ladies, and I am not very likely to do so it appears, as it does not seem to be the custom here, even for the wives of Henry's Spanish friends, to call upon me. They do not appear to be what we should call a hospitable people, though in their own way, I believe, they are so. Mrs. D—— told me that, after living for six years in Spain, she had never been asked into a Spanish house; and that, though always ready to accept your invitations, they never return them. Except for a few balls in the winter, Madrid is not a gay place. Dinner-parties or ordinary evening-parties are unknown; tertulias are the only approach to the latter, but to them the ladies go in morning-dress, and no refreshment is ever given, except sugar and water.

Every one has a box or stall at the opera and some of the theatres, and they attend night after night, with all the regularity of a religious duty, and in the long intervals between the acts visit their friends in the other parts of the house.

I do not find the Spaniards so courteous as they get credit for. Certainly they have a number of little surface politenesses about which they are very punctilious; and, if bows count for anything, they are a most polite nation. A Spanish gentleman, who knows you, will make no end of flattering speeches, no end of bows, and will place everything he has at your disposal; but if you meet him as a stranger in the street or travelling, you will probably meet with something very much the reverse of politeness. He will elbow you on the pavement, and make you go off into the mud, while he keeps the wall side; to say nothing of staring you out of countenance, for that, I believe, they do not consider rude. Among the lower orders it is, of course, much worse. The roughest English navvy treats a lady with respect, and we have frequently met with true politeness from them in our country walks, when we have been in any difficulty; but I do not believe a Spanish peasant would put out his finger to help you, whatever happened. They seem to take a special delight in trying to frighten my horse, and as soon think of flying as calling off a dog of theirs, if it attacks me. The other day I was riding with Mr. A——, and coming into Madrid we met two men rolling some casks along the road. The casks were empty and were making a great noise, and naturally frightened the horses, which both turned suddenly round; we turned them again, and drew to the side of the road; but the casks were immediately rolled over in front of us again. Just then a horse that was before us became so terrified that it reared violently, threw its rider, and came galloping past us. Mr. A—— very quietly asked the men to stop for a moment, while the lady passed, as my horse would do nothing but rear and turn round and round; but they only laughed and set the casks rolling again, I suppose with the hope of seeing me come off next. We were obliged to turn into a side road. Nor is this by any means an isolated case; the same sort of thing is happening every day; and I must say, that amongst the roughest Lancashire workmen I never met with incivility of this sort.

I told you that it was not the custom here for ladies to go out anywhere alone; but even with another lady, or sometimes even a gentleman, you do not avoid annoyance in passing through the streets. Indeed the "pollos" generally seize the opportunity, when, from the narrowness of the pavement you are obliged to separate for a moment from the gentleman who is with you, to accost you, trusting that you will say nothing about it rather than make a disturbance. This annoyance has become so notorious in Madrid that the papers have taken it up, and are constantly writing about it. When Mrs. —— and I have been out together, we have thought it was because we were English, but it seems the Spanish ladies are just as much annoyed. And yet these very men in your own house would be the quintessence of politeness, and would make you bows enough to last an Englishman a lifetime. Some of their little points of etiquette are curious enough; for instance, a Spaniard will always refuse anything you offer him; and you are expected to press him till he takes it. I am always forgetting this when I offer them tea, and leaving them without, because they say "No." It is a mark of politeness, too, to offer you something off their own plates, which you must not refuse. This is a most disagreeable custom. In coming in or out of a railway carriage or any public place, you must bow to all the company, which is a horrible nuisance at a *table d'hôte*, as they leave the table one after another, and keep you nodding like a mandarin. They look upon you as an English boor if you do not. Ladies never rise to receive a guest, as we do; but a gentleman leaving a lady's presence makes a series of bows from her to the door, and turns round to make a final reverence as he goes out. I never feel quite sure they are not coming back by-and-by to make another. They greet you with, "A los pies de V., Señora" ("At your feet, Señora"); and when you meet any of the servants going about the house, they always say, "Que pase V. bien, Señora" ("May you pass well"). The servants, too, always call each other señor or señora. And I heard two little ragged children quarrelling in the street the other day in the most polite style. "No, Señor," one was saying; "Si, Señor," the other was answering, all the time that they were on the point of fighting; and their united height was about five feet and a half. Every one has heard of the Spanish habit of placing everything at your disposal, without the slightest intention of your accepting anything. When writing to you, if they speak of their own house they call it, "En esta su casa de V." ("This, your house"); but these little filigree politenesses really mean nothing, and do not proceed from delicacy of feeling or kindliness of heart, and, therefore, are found in conjunction with extreme rudeness and coarseness. I must say that my experience so far of Spaniards is, that they are not a courteous nation, in the true sense of the word. At the same time, among the better class of the lower orders, there is a pleasant, friendly manner, which is very attractive, and even a sort of natural politeness; and as Spaniards never know what it is to feel shy, they are at home in any company and, therefore, never awkward.

We have beautiful weather now, while I suppose you Londoners are enveloped in thick yellow fogs. From about nine o'clock in the morning till five in the afternoon it is almost too hot. You could not remain in the sun without getting a headache in the middle of the day, but the mornings are sometimes colder than I ever felt it in the middle of winter in England. It is a curious kind of cold too; you do not notice it at first, but it seems to paralyse you and make your very bones ache, and no amount of clothing seems to keep it out. The trees are still green; only some of the acacias are in the sere and yellow leaf.

Our visits to Toledo and the Escorial are veritable *châteaux en Espagne,* for they melt into thin air, whenever the day we fix for them arrives.

November 12.

We have had no letters from any of you for nearly a fortnight. I can only hope that no news is good news. We are in a flourishing state of health, and are rejoicing in our English energy, which takes us out these cold mornings for a good gallop, while these miserable Spaniards are soaking in bed, and those few whom a cruel fate has compelled to turn out, are rolled up to the eyes in their cloaks, and creep along in the sun, looking like mummies partially revived. They are as frightened of a breath of air as if they were built of cards, and are always terrified of catching "pulmonía" (inflammation of the lungs). It is certainly a terrible disease here, carrying people off in a few hours; but it is no wonder, for they keep themselves stewing in these cloaks with their mouths completely covered, until they are in a sort of vapour-bath; and then, perhaps, meeting a friend in the street, down comes the cloak for a few minutes, and the icy wind from the Guadarramas catches them and deals them a deathblow; or they parboil themselves in steaming cafés, and go home in the bitter morning air; so it is no wonder they catch cold.

HOW SPANIARDS CATCH "PULMONÍA."

And once down with pulmonía the doctors soon bleed them to death. Among the women, who go very lightly clad and with nothing over their heads, there is a very small percentage of deaths from this complaint.

How the babies live is my wonder. They wear the same kind of swaddling-clothes that were fashionable in the time of Herod. The baby is placed at the end of a long piece of coarse flannel, the colour of mustard,—all the Spanish flannel appears to be this intense yellow, and as thick as a blanket,—and rolled up to the top, leaving nothing but its head out, then it is pinned quite tightly, and looks like a young mummy. They are, of course, perfectly stiff, so that you could rear them up on end in a corner; but how the mothers carry them I cannot imagine. They have a disgusting habit, too, of never washing a child's head until it is about two years old, so you may imagine what the poor little wretches look like,—though, to be sure, they do wear caps. They appear to be kept up all night, for you see numbers of young children of two or three years old at the theatres, or on the Prado, at night until twelve o'clock, and they are, consequently, the most sickly, withered-looking little creatures, whose age it would be impossible to guess, as they look like dwarfed old men and women. The little **girls of the upper class are** put into stiff stays and high-heeled boots, so that you never see them playing as children ought to do. Sometimes they make a ghastly attempt at skipping, but generally walk along by their nurse's side with their legs growing out and their ankles in, owing to their tight boots, and their waists pinched in like a wasp. I cannot bear to see them. Almost the only game among the boys seems to be bull-fighting; they have large heads made of wicker-work, and one boy putting on a bull's head acts the part of "toro," while the others personate horses and picadores.

Nothing strikes you more in Spain than the utter worthlessness of time; smoking a paper cigar is exertion enough for a Spaniard, and even that must be done leisurely. An English friend of ours who is staying here says, that if you want to take the spirit once for all out of a man, and teach him uncomplaining patience, let him come to Madrid. If you are going by railway, you must be at the station half an hour before the train starts, or you will not be allowed to take a ticket (Spaniards are always there a full hour before). And when the train does start, it will stop at each little roadside station —even when there is not a single passenger to get out or in—for three-quarters of an hour, while all the porters, station-master, guards, engine-driver, etc., light their cigarettes and have a nice quiet smoke. If you take a cab, and it is of any importance to arrive at your destination by a certain time, you frequently have to get out again and walk, because you can do it so much more quickly than the horse; and, in short, if you are in a hurry, there is nothing to be done but come out of it again, for it is easier for a camel to go through the eye of a needle than for a Madrileño to exert himself; and all his movements, compared with an Englishman, are as of those of the hour-hand to the minute-hand of a clock. I suppose it is to show their supreme indifference to the value of time, that their great clock in the Puerta del Sol shows a different hour on each of its three faces. I have frequently seen ten minutes between them.

We went to the opera last night to hear Patti in

'Sonnambula.' I was charmed with her; but I wonder that any good artiste will sing in this theatre; for the people certainly do not know how to behave. Half the house will begin to applaud violently, wishing for an encore, and the other half will hiss as violently to put a stop to it, until the opera is quite at a standstill, and no one can be heard at all. If the encore is not given, every singer is hissed off the stage if they attempt to continue the piece; and if it is given, the opposition party make such a noise that you cannot hear it. To add to my pleasure, I had a little " pollo " behind me, who hummed most audibly all the most delicate airs as Patti was singing; and the people in the boxes always talk as loudly as ever they can, so that you have to listen to an opera under considerable difficulties in Madrid.

Ladies go in morning-dress to the stalls, which occupy all the pit; but in the boxes they sometimes dress most gorgeously. I saw a duchess the other evening in grass-green satin, with necklace, bracelets, earrings, and stomacher of diamonds, and, besides all these, an enormous bracelet of the same round the top of each of her exceedingly substantial arms above the elbow, and a tiara on her head, with a large tuft that looked like spun glass, but may have been brilliants, sticking out in the front, like the things the volunteers wear in their shakos. She looked a little barbaric, I must confess.

November 20, 1863.

We have decided to go to Valencia at last, and I think we shall start next week, so you must not be surprised if you do not receive any letters for some little time, as it is so difficult to write when travelling. We shall not remain very long, as we must be back before Christmas. I am rather anxious to go where I hear there are trees and flowers. The country about here does not, however, look quite so dreary now, as the wheat is up, and the fields are green here and there.

We had a grand review the other day; but, indeed, we are always having grand reviews or parading of the troops, in one shape or another. They do not seem to do much, but spread them all along the Prado, and then march them to barracks with indescribable beatings of drums, and general clashing of other instruments. They have a very fine brigade of mountain artillery; at least, those who know anything about it say it is very fine. The guns are small, and are carried on the backs of very splendid mules, so that they can be taken anywhere about the mountains in case of necessity. The other troops seem to me to consist of the merest boys, very dirty and slovenly-looking.

The mules and donkeys are certainly very fine, especially the former. Many people drive them in their carriages, and for night-work they are excellent, as they do not take cold. They are clipped so curiously. Only the upper part of the animal is shaved, leaving the long winter coat on its legs, and halfway up its body. Generally on the shoulder, and above the tail, there is a pattern made, by leaving some of the hair a little longer, so that it appears as if embossed in velvet on the skin. I believe the trade of clipping is in the hands of the gipsies, and certainly they do it most beautifully. The other day I saw a donkey with "*viva mi amo*" (long life to my master) left in this way across his back, and a beautiful scroll pattern on each side. While we were standing behind it looking at it, the master called out from a shop that the donkey would kick if we went too near. I do not know whether this elaborate clipping had been done with a view of playing a practical joke on any one who was curious enough to go within reach of his heels to examine it.

Apropos of gipsy clippers, I heard a story the other day. One of these men was going along a country road, when he saw a gentleman sitting on the bank by the roadside, and near him one of the little white poodles which are so common in Spain. The gipsy stopped. "Buenos dias, caballero," said he. "Buenos dias," replied the gentleman. "That is a nice little dog," remarked the gipsy. "Yes, he is not bad," returned the other. "Don't you think he would look better if he were clipped?" insinuated the gipsy. "Well, I dare say he would." "Shall I clip him?" asked the man. "Yes, clip him by all means." The gipsy set to work at the poodle, and in a short time had made him look quite lion-like. "Don't you think he would look nice with ruffs round his legs?" asked the gipsy by-and-by. "Yes, I think he would," returned the gentleman. "And on his tail?"—"Yes; put one on his tail if you like."—"Shall I put him a moustache?" was the next question. "And a pair of eyebrows?" The gentleman agreed, and the decoration of the poodle proceeded. At last it was finished, and the dog set at liberty. "Does he not look nice now?" remarked the gipsy; "he is quite a different creature." And a very different creature poor poodle seemed to think himself, for after turning round two or three times, as if with the hope of getting a better view of himself, he seemed to be in such a puzzle about his own identity, that he scampered off, probably to make inquiries of some of his canine friends.

The gipsy held out his hand for payment, saying complacently, "Two dollars, Señor, if you please." "Two dollars! what for?" asked the gentleman with a look of astonishment. "For shaving the little dog, Señor," replied the gipsy with a grin. "It is not my dog," quietly replied the gentleman; "it was sleeping here when I came by."

LETTER V.

MADRID, *December* 20, 1863.

WE returned from our trip to Valencia on Friday, as Henry had to go north on business before Christmas Day. We left Madrid in the evening, so that we might get over the plains of La Mancha while it was dark. No one who has seen the plains of Castile, and hears that those of La Mancha are still worse, would be mad enough to cross them by daylight, when all their desolation is visible. Soon after sunrise we entered on what appeared fairyland after withered Madrid. The line runs through a rich irrigated valley, amid groves of palms and oranges, and a luxuriant vegetation, which you find everywhere in Spain where there is water.

As you approach Valencia the country becomes even prettier. You see numbers of pretty whitewashed cottages, each with a wooden cross on the gable and a broad black band painted round the basement to prevent their being splashed and dirtied by the rain, and many of them have vines trained on a trellis-work over the door. You can scarcely imagine what a contrast it is to treeless Castile, where the few houses that are to be seen are mere mud hovels and look more like cattle-sheds than human habitations. Yet pretty, in the sense in which we understand the word in England, it can scarcely be called, because irrigated ground is always so stiff and formal. The vegetation looks very strange, and Henry says is quite like the tropics. The hedges are all of aloes, but you would scarcely recognize them to be the same plant as the miserable, sickly things we have in England; they make a perfectly impenetrable hedge with their enormous prickly leaves, and the flowers rise on a large stalk to the height of a good-sized lime- or chestnut-tree. There are whole fields of that small pink cactus which is so common in our greenhouses—it is used for feeding the cochineal insects,—and quantities of mulberry-trees for the silk-worms. Then, there are the orange-groves which I had been so anxious to see and which are very beautiful, with their glossy dark leaves and golden fruit, and here and there a clump of date-palms or a banana, looking so strangely foreign. I felt like a bird suddenly let loose into the fields after being shut up for months in a cage in a dingy back parlour.

We arrived in Valencia about twelve o'clock. It is a much more characteristically Spanish town than Madrid, having less of the modern French style about it than the capital. The people, too, are fresher and better-looking than the Madrileños, which can hardly fail to be the case when you know in what a different climate and landscape they live. The national dress of the Valencians—at least of the men—is very odd. They wear short white trousers, which scarcely reach to the knees, and are so wide that from behind they look like a woman's petticoat, being plaited thickly at the back; a white shirt with a crimson *faja*, or sash, rolled round the waist; no stockings, but sandals made of a kind of grass and tied on with black ribbon; and a red woollen nightcap completes their dress in warm weather. When it is colder, they add a black cloth waistcoat without sleeves,

VALENCIANO IN WINTER COSTUME.

left open, a pair of rude leather gaiters, fastened at the ankle and the knee and gaping between, and a blue and white "manta," which generally is only thrown across one shoulder, but sometimes put on something like a Scotch plaid, only that the end is thrown over the left shoulder in such a way as to cover the mouth. Their hair is cut quite short, and the head tightly bound up in a red handkerchief. The women wear short petticoats and a little shawl crossed over the breast and pinned behind, and their hair is all combed straight back from the face and coiled in plaits at the back; it gives you the idea that they cannot shut their eyes. Among the higher classes you see no bonnets, as in Madrid, and the women are very much prettier. We spent some time in the cathedral and ascended the tower, from whence there is a fine view of the city, which looks curiously Eastern, with its flat roofs and strange shining tiles. This was the first Spanish cathedral I had seen, as there is none in Madrid, and our long-talked-of visit to Toledo is still in the future. It is not to be compared, I believe, to Seville, or most of the others, but I found it very interesting.

We also spent one delightful day at the Albufera de Valencia,—an immense marsh or, as it really is, a shallow lake, twenty-seven miles in circumference. We took a tartana—a kind of covered waggonette without springs, but with seats slung with broad leather straps, which have very much the same effect,—and with a couple of splendid Valencian horses, were soon spinning over the ground, past the neat little vine-covered cottages, scattered so thickly over the country as to give a very homelike appearance to it,—groves of orange- and lemon-trees, with their burdens of fruit, and vast fields of maize and cactus, with occasional palms and bananas. After some time we came to the rice-fields, which are all sunk below the level of the road and were covered with water. They are by no means pretty in their present state, but I was glad to have an idea of a rice swamp. The country about here is, however, so extremely unhealthy that in summer the villages are entirely deserted, no one daring to face the fever and ague which would be the certain result of remaining in them. For this reason no one is allowed to grow rice without a special licence, and I believe no new grounds are now permitted. The cottages we passed on our way were models of neatness, with their rows of brightly-polished pans and clean crockery, as we could see through the wide door, which is large enough to admit a carriage, and is always left open during the day. At last we came to a deserted-looking village on the edge of the lake. More than half the houses were shut up, and scarcely a soul was to be seen about the streets. I believe during last summer this place was completely depopulated; those few who did not fly from the malaria having died of fever. Now that the weather was cooler some two or three had returned to their cottages, but they looked only half alive, and only seemed to make the desolation more striking. Here we took a boat,—a long shallow black gondola-looking affair, with a very high, pointed prow, which the boatman pushed along by planting a long pole in the bottom of the lake, and running from stem to stern. The water is about six or seven feet deep in the deepest parts, and is so beautifully clear as to show every pebble and weed lying at the bottom. It was a glorious day, and we lay back in the boat enjoying the *dolce far niente* to the uttermost. The Albufera is covered with wildfowl of every description. The shooting over it belongs at present to General Prim, and a man named Campos, who has made a great fortune in railways, I believe. When the Empress was here the other day, they had a chair fitted up for her use on one of the islands, of reeds, and as the wildfowl were driven past her she shot them,—rather an ignominious kind of sport, I think. The borders of the lake are covered with trees and a thick undergrowth of evergreen oak, and a plant which looks like a myrtle, but bears a bright scarlet berry about the size of a hazel-nut. The scene was very beautiful: the lake is so large that the villages on the opposite shore looked mere white specks, and in one direction there was no boundary to be seen, only the water stretching away to meet the sky. We landed, and spent a long time wandering about under the trees, and sitting on the moss enjoying the view, and returned to Valencia in the cool of the evening.

There is a most curious tribunal in Valencia for the settlement of disputes about the water on irrigated land. It has existed, I believe, ever since the time of the Moors, and from it there is no appeal. Every Thursday, three of the oldest men in the city, chosen specially for the office, seat themselves on the steps of a particular door of the cathedral, and to them come all the disputants and state their respective complaints and defences. This done, the old men put their heads under one cloak, and consult about the judgment. When they have agreed, they uncover their heads and announce their decision. We unfortunately missed this curious sight, but a friend of ours who did see it was very much amused. The judges sentenced a man to pay a certain fine, and he immediately began to argue against the sentence, saying, "But, Señores—" "Pay another peseta for speaking," said the old men. "But, Señores, I—" "Una peseta mas," solemnly returned the judge; and finding that every word he spoke cost him "una peseta mas," he soon gave up and retired. Report says, however, that the water-quarrels are oftener settled by the knife than in any other way; and those who live in Valencia do not give the people a good name.

We made a little excursion along the coast, stopping at Castellon de la Plana. On our way in the train we passed Murviedro, the ancient Saguntum, a most interesting old place, apparently, and full of Roman remains. It is magnificently situated on the top of a high rock, overlooking the whole valley below. We had not time, unfortunately, to spend a day there as we had intended. Castellon is a very ordinary Spanish village about three miles from the sea, standing in the midst of gardens and orange-groves. We stayed at the Fonda del Progreso; and a most wretched place it is, with a bare, miserable *table-d'hôte*-room, with a rickety table and some crazy chairs, and a floor on which the waiters are accustomed to empty the dregs of the glasses and the remnants of the dishes. There were four Spaniards seated at the opposite end of the table to us, who gobbled up their own dinners, and then leaned upon their elbows and watched us, while they picked and sucked their teeth,—ladies and all. We had a tureen of greasy hot-water, with large lumps of bread in it, for soup. I believe it was what the "puchero" was boiled in, and the puchero itself was served afterwards on a dish. It consists principally of "garbanzos" (a small bean), peas, cabbage, chicken-bones, bacon, etc. etc.,—a regular *omnium gatherum*, strongly flavoured with garlic. This is the universal dish in Spain, on which both gentle and simple live; I cannot say it is particularly tempting to an English palate. The wine is simply disgusting, having the strongest possible flavour of the dirty pig-skin in which it is kept.

In the morning we started off to Torre Blanca, where Henry wished to see a marsh that is in course of draining by an English company. The drive from Castellon is very beautiful. The road runs between the mountains and the sea, through park-like-looking ground covered with cork- and algaroba-trees. The last bear the locust bean, on which, I suppose, John the Baptist fed; and if so, I am sure he must have been very plump and comfortable-looking, for they are as sweet as dates, and have very much the same taste. The horses and mules are all fed on them here, and they are as fat as possible and have the most beautifully glossy coats. By-and-by the road ascends and rounds a headland which juts out into the sea. From this point there is a beautiful view across the blue, glistening Mediterranean, and back to Castellon, lying on the other side of the little bay, with its fringe of white, tiny, wavelets breaking on the sand. After passing round this headland, we came upon the scene of a sad accident which happened about two years ago. One terribly stormy night, when all the torrents were swollen by the rain, the diligence from Barcelona stopped at a little village named Oropesa, a few miles from this spot, to change horses. The villagers tried to persuade the mayoral to put up for the night, as they declared it was not safe to attempt to cross the streams on such a night. The mayoral, however, was not to be deterred by fear of danger; and two young Englishmen who were passengers, ashamed, I suppose, to be less courageous than he, determined to go on also. They started, and immediately after leaving the village, overtook two of the civil guards whose duty it is to patrol the roads all night. The mayoral offered them a seat, and they mounted the coach. Nothing more was ever heard of the diligence or its unfortunate cargo. Not arriving in Castellon the next day, a messenger was dispatched to discover the cause, and the villagers set out to try and find some trace of the missing vehicle. Of the coach itself nothing was ever discovered; but one of the horses was found uninjured, and grazing quietly on the seashore, close to the mouth of a mountain-stream swollen by the rain to a furious torrent. Afterwards some of the bodies were thrown up on the shore at a great distance. The two Englishmen were buried in a small piece of ground bought by their friends and enclosed for that purpose at Oropesa; and a monument was erected to the memory of the two civil guards on what was supposed to be the scene of the catastrophe.

The theory is that the diligence had been carried bodily out to sea while crossing the torrent, over which there is no bridge, and which it must, therefore, have forded. We left the carriage to look at the place, but, as the ravine through which the stream runs is narrow and covered with underwood, and trees which meet and interlace over it, it seems impossible that a large diligence, with all its pile of luggage, could have been carried through these trees without leaving some traces. What seems more probable is, that it had passed the stream and ascended the headland, and that in rounding the point where the road hangs quite perpendicularly over the sea, the horses had either missed their way and gone straight over the precipice, or had become terrified and overturned the diligence, and so been dragged over. This would account for the one horse being found uninjured, and for the total disappearance of the coach without leaving any trace. However it happened, it was very sad, and we looked with much interest at the harmless-looking little brook now babbling along so innocently and gently, and at the two lonely graves of the young Englishmen, which we passed a little further on at Oropesa—a place with a curious old tower, in which, it is said, the Moors used to receive the tribute which they obliged the Spaniards to pay.

On leaving Castellon, among the mountains on our left, we had passed a curious little whitewashed church, dedicated to St. Mary Magdalen. There is a legend connected with it that the town of Castellon was originally built round this church in the mountains; but, as the people found this situation very inconvenient, they prayed earnestly to their patron saint, who, very goodnaturedly, one night, while they were all asleep, carried the whole town down to the plain, whence it is still called Castellon de la Plana. She, however, seems to have preferred the more airy residence for herself, and so left her chapel where it was; so, on her day, her faithful servants make a pilgrimage to visit her in great state. I should like to see this procession very much, for it must be a curious one. In Spanish villages which are too poor to have wooden images of their saints, living people personate the sacred characters, and on this day the procession is headed by a girl, who is chosen for her beauty, but not for her modesty or good character, and who, gaudily dressed and covered with jewellery, rides in a cart, which is decorated with flowers: she represents the Magdalen in the days of her sin. The girl is allowed to keep the dress and the ornaments, so there is no difficulty in finding some one to play the part; and as the men are allowed to say anything they like to her, and generally attend her cart in crowds, the scene must be more curious than edifying. Behind her comes a cart containing another young girl, also chosen for her beauty, but of unblemished character. She is very simply dressed; and the part is very popular, as they say that every girl who takes the part of the penitent Magdalen is married before the year is out. Lastly comes a wooden figure of Christ on the cross, and Mary weeping at the foot, dressed in deep mourning. This part is played by a respectable married woman or widow. The priests conduct the procession, followed by the whole village, to the church on the mountain, where they perform Mass, and return in the evening,—generally, I believe, after a day spent in rather wild orgies.

Further up these same mountains there is a large monastery, only just visible from the road. The monks in this place are, I believe, the only ones in Spain who are allowed to wear the habit of their order. At the time of the suppression of the monasteries this favour was granted to them, because they had been so charitable in succouring the wounded on both sides in the Carlist wars. Scattered over the mountain-top, around the convent, are numbers of little whitewashed huts, each with a bell outside on the roof. These, I believe, are, or have been, occupied by Trappist monks; but, as they die off, their places are not filled up, and the huts are left empty. I do not know if they are in connection with the large monastery or not, but the inhabitants of these huts hold no communication with any one. At matins each brother rings his bell, and it is only when this ceases to be heard at the accustomed time that one of the other monks goes to his hut, generally to find him dying or dead. This is at least what I was told; but you can never vouch for the truth of any story you hear in Spain.

Further on, the road recedes still more from the sea, and lies altogether among the mountains. The scenery is very beautiful, as all mountain scenery is, and occasionally we would catch a glimpse of the sapphire blue of the Mediterranean, and of Castellon in the extreme distance, looking quite pretty among its orange-groves. From the highest ridge of hills, we came in sight of a beautiful little bay, with the marsh, which was our destination, lying at the edge of the sea, between it and a richly-cultivated ground. We spent several hours wandering about on the sea-shore, and under the cork-trees, and dined in a little venta, which had been a monastery, with a picture of San Antonio over the door. We had wisely brought our own provisions. It was difficult to believe we were almost at Christmas, in that balmy, delicious air, and warm sunshine. The people told us it was never much colder than this at any time of the year. A great part of the ground was covered with palmitos, a small plant, which grows about a couple of feet high, and looks like the crest of a miniature palm. While I was looking at one of these, an old labourer, wearing the curious costume which I have already described, pulled one up by the roots, and, cutting away all the outer leaves, presented it to me, telling me it was good to eat; and so, indeed, I found it: it looked and tasted like a new almond, and I believe it forms a regular article of food among the country people. We had to ride down to the marsh on donkeys, as it was at some distance, lying between the road and the sea. To my ignorant eyes, it did not look at all like a marsh, being covered with bushes, and we were guided along a path which was perfectly firm. My steed was a very good one; but I had nothing in the

VALENCIAN, WITH PALMITO.

shape of a saddle but a sheepskin tied across the animal, and for a bridle a piece of rope, which was knotted round his nose, and came up on one side of his head, so that when I wanted him to go to the left, I could pull the rope; but when he was to go to the right, I had to box his ear on the opposite side. At last I managed to have a rope, with a loop to it fastened to the sheepskin, by way of a stirrup, and then I could trot quite independently, without any fear of tumbling off in a fit of laughter, as I had been in imminent danger of doing before.

SELF AND STEED.

And no wonder; for some of the gentlemen of our party kept slipping off behind, or in front, or at the side of their donkeys, at every second step, more especially as the animals kept making rushes under the cork-trees by way of ridding themselves of their burdens, and as the patent bridles were not very effective, it was very difficult to prevent their doing so.

We found the drainage works were only just commenced, so there was not much to be seen, but we enjoyed a ramble along the shore.

It was evening when we started again for Castellon, and on ascending the hill had a beautiful view of the little bay we had just left in all the changing beauty of a fine sunset. The Mediterranean certainly deserves its character of a sapphire sea. The water seems of a peculiarly beautiful blue, the colour of the flame of sulphur; but it looks only like a huge lake with its tideless waves and placid ripple, though I suppose it is stormy enough sometimes.

When we began to descend the mountains towards Castellon, we found our horse very much given to saying his prayers; and as it was a beautiful moonlight night, and as balmy as midsummer, we agreed to walk on and let the devout animal follow at his leisure. I never enjoyed anything more than this walk, for the scenery looked perfectly bewitching in the moonlight; and, to add to the effect, on the steep mountain-side on our right were numbers of caves, inhabited at present by the workmen who are employed on the new railway to Barcelona, which is now in course of construction. These caves were all lighted up inside, and in front of some you could see strange, wild-looking figures thrown out in strong relief against the ruddy glare of the fire-light; others had torn pieces of matting hung before them. It gave one a bogyish feeling, which added considerably to the pleasure of the walk, especially as we had heard that within a very few years those caves had been the lurking-places of bandits, who would not have left us long in such quiet enjoyment of the picturesque.

We walked so much faster than our pious horse that we had to wait half an hour at the turnpike for the tartana, and did not reach the hotel until nearly ten o'clock. We found the streets of the town all crowded, as it was one of the numerous days of the Virgin. We met the procession as we entered the principal street, and were obliged to go round by some of the narrow lanes to avoid it.

One thing that amused me very much was the attention I excited among the country people. Whenever we changed horses during our day's excursion we were obliged to leave the tartana, as,

VALENCIAN VILLAGER INSPECTING THE NEW CURIOSITY.

from some beautiful contrivance or other, the thing had to be turned almost wrong side up before the horse could be got out; and as it was a grand fiesta all the people were out in the streets of the villages. They surrounded me in a body, walking round me as if I were a wild beast, grinning and talking to each other in their curious *patois*, which is unintelligible to a Castellano. I suppose they had never seen a lady in a hat before, for mine seemed to cause them unbounded astonishment, and

HIDALGO IN GALA COSTUME.

they came so close to me, in their anxiety to examine it, that I thought they were going to feel if I were alive. They looked very much like savages, I must say, with their long inanimate faces and lustreless eyes, and they are as dark as Indians. The greater part of them appeared absolutely devoid of intelligence. These are the labourers; the better class of men were dressed in long black cloaks, as glossy as satin, and wide, straight-brimmed felt hats, with a small steeple crown, on the edge of which was a black silk tuft, as well as on the brim, which had a narrow binding of velvet, turned up. They looked like so many serious old crows, as they solemnly paced up and down the streets, "tomando el sol." It looked altogether rather a melancholy sort of fiesta. It is curious how many of the Valencianos have fair hair, and among the children you see as many white heads as in the north of Ireland. There is a very strong mixture of French in their dialect, which is a very strange one to listen to.

The next day we drove down to the sea through gardens of orange- and lemon-trees and bananas, and had a kind of picnic in a pine-grove there. I found numbers of wild-flowers; dark blue forget-me-nots, and a beautiful little immortelle, which grows in little, white, satiny tufts, and another flower, about the size of a dog-rose, but with a bright amber or crimson centre,—I think it must be some kind of cistus. Aloes also we saw growing wild close to the water's edge. I was very anxious to eat an orange freshly plucked from the tree; but I was told they were not ripe, though they looked so. The crop for the English market is already gathered; we saw waggons full of boxes at the station. We were told that the finest flavoured oranges all go to England; they are a smaller kind, and ripen first. Next comes a large, coarse-skinned orange, which is sent to France, as they say the French care more for size than quality; and the Spanish crop is the latest, and, I believe, the worst.

We returned to Valencia the same evening, and spent the next day wandering about the "city of the Cid," leaving for Madrid in the evening so as to pass La Mancha before daylight. In the middle of the night we all awoke almost simultaneously and found the train standing still. We felt as if we had had a very long, comfortable sleep without any jolting and were congratulating each other, when suddenly the idea struck me that our carriage had become detached from the train, and that we were left behind somewhere on the road. We looked out;—no station, no lights to be seen! It was pitch dark, so that we actually could not see whether there were any train or not. Henry jumped out in a fright, and found it was all there with the exception of the engine, which had broken down, and some one had been dispatched to the next station to fetch another. We had already been waiting two hours, though we had happily been asleep and had known nothing about it. About a quarter of an hour afterwards, the engine arrived and we started again; but in the morning we pulled up at an utterly dreary-looking little station and waited for half an hour. Henry asked what we were stopping for. "Because there is a train coming out of Madrid, and we might run into it." As there was only a single line of rails, this seemed a very likely contingency. An hour passed. Henry tried again: "Where is the Madrid train?" No one knew. We ought to pass it at Aranjuez, some distance further on, but as we were two hours late, they were afraid it would have started. Another half-hour! We were getting hungry. "Why do you not telegraph?"—"The telegraph is out of order."—"But most likely the other train is waiting for us at Aranjuez."—"Quien

RAILWAY GUARD IN NIGHT COSTUME.

sabe?" was the quiet reply. We appeared likely to spend the day here; it was nine o'clock, and we were to have been in Madrid at half-past seven! At last we began to creep along, whistling and howling like a soul in purgatory, and arrived in course of time at Aranjuez, where we found the other train waiting, and were greeted by the passengers with loud cheers. We arrived in Madrid, half-starved, four hours behind time; but that is nothing in Spain.

CHRISTMAS DAY, 1863.

It seems strange to be writing this date on a warm, sunny, almost summerlike day; but I believe we shall not be able to count upon our fine weather much longer. I suppose you are all shivering over huge fires, or enveloped in a pea-soup fog and feeling rather dismal, as, indeed, nearly every one does on Christmas Day, except children and those happy families which have not yet become scattered over the face of the earth. I have been thinking of you all day, and wishing we could have been with you, but it was impossible; and I do not think now we shall leave before the carnival, which falls about the 11th of February this year.

Christmas time here is much the same as in England, especially in the matter of Christmas-boxes. Every tradesman's assistant, and assistant's assistant, who can possibly have done anything for you during the year, comes with a card of congratulation which has an ulterior purpose. The house has been besieged all day, and even the children of the porter sent up a highly-decorated piece of paper containing a superior poem on the joyful occasion, and waited for their "tip." The streets are very lively. The Plaza Mayor—a large square with colonnades, round it, a sort of dingy Palais Royal—is a perfect fair, full of toys and sweetmeats. On every side you meet large droves of turkeys clacking about in a demented style, as if depressed with dismal forebodings. The children wander about in troops, beating drums and singing wonderful songs about the Nativity. Last night they were informing the public, in a doggrel rhyme, that the Virgin had already been taken ill, and that her confinement was likely to take place in the morning. At some of the small theatres they act religious dramas of the Nativity, apparently just like the old mysteries, on *Noche Buena* (Christmas Eve). This is really the great day, though it is supposed to be a fast. At twelve o'clock at night there is what they called a *Misa de gallo* (cock's Mass), and after that they have a great supper, and then dance and make as much noise as possible till all hours,— one of our neighbours had a barrel-organ in his drawing-room, and nearly drove us mad.

For our part, we had a party of twelve to dinner, and the evening passed off very well. My pudding and mincemeat were a great success, which you would wonder at if you knew the difficulty I had in getting anything to make them with.

Henry helped me to write for what I wanted, and we did very well with the fruit; but when we came to the spices we were at a standstill. The receipt said mace, so we looked out the Spanish word and wrote down on the list the quantity we required. Suddenly I bethought me of looking out in the English part of the dictionary the translation of the Spanish word, to be quite sure we were right: I found we had ordered one ounce of "the baton of office carried before a mayor." However, at last we managed to get most of the ingredients, but were obliged to dispense with the spices, as they are never used in Spanish cookery, and are, therefore, not to be had. The raisins and currants are most inferior to what we have in England, and candied fruit is unknown; so I was obliged to use preserved limes and oranges, which answered very well. The Spaniards have several kinds of sweets which seem to be peculiar to this time of year, and old Canuto, Henry's servant and majordomo, seemed to think it necessary to produce them all for my especial benefit.

The principal one is made in a round, flat paper-box, about eighteen inches in diameter, and consists of a layer of some kind of cake spread upon wafer-paper, then a layer of preserves, then almond-icing, and finally sugar-icing, like a bride's cake,—altogether about two inches deep. The top is decorated with candied cherries, apricots, plums, etc., and sugar ornaments filled with liqueur. They are fearfully rich, as you may imagine, and proportionately indigestible. They are generally sent as presents; we received a very splendid one, which was handed round after dinner.

I have been going round some of the churches in Madrid lately, and wretched places they are. The principal one is supposed to be that of San Isidro, who is the patron saint of the city, but none of them are worth looking at. The one which the Queen patronizes is that of the Atocha, at the end of the Prado. It looks like a German toy, and is as dreary inside as it is ugly outside, which is saying a great deal. It is, however, the dwelling-place of a very celebrated Virgin who performs great miracles, and to whom all the royal children are specially presented as soon as they are old enough to be taken out. She is as black as coal, and appears to have nothing but a head; and her clothes are held out by three sticks, like a gipsy's tent. She is, certainly, the most undignified idol I ever saw, notwithstanding that her dresses are most gorgeous, being generally the cast-off clothes of her Most Catholic Majesty, who goes in grand state to visit her whenever she has a new baby to present, or a victory to return thanks for; on a Saturday afternoon, too, while in town, she always performs her devotions at this shrine.

At one of the side altars, the wall is completely covered with votive offerings; and a very heterogeneous and nasty collection they are, principally consisting of wax or plaster models of diseased arms and legs, or crooked backs, which this most amiable saint has cured; old clothes, crutches, slings, shades for the eyes, bandages, etc. etc. Among other things, I noticed two babies' coffins, a splendid head of woman's hair, and any amount of odd shoes, boots, stockings, and clothes, principally children's. What puzzled me was the coffins. Had they been ordered in anticipation of some sickly children's death, and presented to the Virgin when they became useless? Or, as they were pink, and very highly decorated, were they merely hung there for ornament?

Talking of coffins, though, they have a curious way of conducting funerals here. In the first place, the coffins are always some bright colour,— generally pink or magenta,—and gaudily ornamented with brass nails and filigree-work; the lid is very much raised in the centre, and is fastened with two wretched locks instead of being screwed down. The hearse or car in which the body is taken to the cemetery, is very like one of those circus-cars which you see driving in processions round country towns, gaudy and tawdry to a degree, and flaming in yellow and red. The horses that draw it are bedizened in the same style, with crimson and gold housings thrown over them reaching to the ground. The cemeteries are large square courts or gardens, surrounded by a roofed wall about six feet deep, which is all honeycombed like the niches in an escritoire; these holes are the graves, and the coffins are pushed into them, feet foremost, and then they are bricked up and cemented at the end. The epitaph is put on this cemented covering, and the effect of a well-filled cemetery is that of a chemist's shop with innumerable drawers, each with a separate label.

At the last moment, just before the coffin is put into the niche, the lid is unlocked, and all those present at the funeral come forward and take a last look at their dead friend; the coffin is then closed, locked, and the keys given to the nearest relative. The corpse is buried in full dress; if an officer, in uniform. The poor people are carried to the cemetery in stretchers with pointed coverings of black tarpauling, with a death's-head and crossbones painted on in white. They are buried in the ground in the centre of the graveyard, and are, I believe, turned out of the coffin, which is only hired to carry the body to the grave. On All Hallows Eve every one goes to visit the tombs of their dead friends, and decorate them with immortelles. On this day the streets are quite deserted, and the roads leading to the Campos Santos are crowded. Few graves are left without a chaplet; on many of them you see a photograph of the deceased hanging in the centre of the tablet. I must confess this way of burying seems to be a most comfortless one; the cemeteries look so like a shop, and so dreary, and I cannot help feeling that some day the walls will crumble away and leave all the bones exposed. Indeed, this had actually happened in a village we passed through the other day, and there was one niche completely filled with odd bones and skulls of all sizes. Our own little English cemetery is very pretty, and is kept in beautiful order, being full of flowers. It is surrounded by high walls, with a tower at each corner, as if it were a fortress. It is only of late years that we have been allowed to have a burial-ground at all. Formerly the people used to dig up the corpse of any Protestant who was buried, and fling it into the ditch; and when any Englishman died, his friend used to have to bury him at night in some secret place,—several people were interred in the gas-works, and one under the stall of a stable.

We are constantly meeting the procession of the Host going to a sick person. There is a custom here that when the priest leaves the church, carrying the holy wafer, he has a right to stop the first carriage or cab he meets, turn out the occupant, and take possession of it himself, and the unfortunate dispossessed is expected to follow on foot to the house of the sick person. The consequence is, that no sooner is the first tinkle of the little bell heard, than every vehicle immediately escapes up the side streets to avoid being pressed into the service of "*Su Magestad,*" as they respectfully call the wafer. Many of the foot-passengers, too, turn aside to avoid meeting the procession, although very few, except old women, go down on their knees as the Host passes. Formerly, however, I believe every one used to drop devoutly on their knees; and they tell of a dreadful scrape an Englishman got into here for refusing to be turned out of his carriage to make way for the priest.

The Queen sometimes edifies the faithful by happening to meet the procession and giving up her carriage and six and walking humbly behind. When this happens, the event is recorded amid much blowing of shawms in the newspapers, and she is called a worthy descendant of Isabel la Católica. I do not know if I have ever told you anything of the Queen. She is exactly like her photographs, except that you must add to them a nose and lips that look as if newly stung by a wasp. The first time I saw her was in the opera, and then she wore a dress of cherry-coloured and black satin, in stripes about six inches wide,—you may imagine it was not very becoming to her.

She has, however, a frank, pleasing expression, which makes you fancy she must have been comely enough when she was young; and her manners are said to be singularly agreeable, and withal queenly. Every one says that after you have been a short time in her company you forget what she is in the charm of her manner. Among the lower classes, and the country people, she is popular, for she is extremely religious,—I use the word advisedly,—and is very generous, and easy of access. This may account for the praise which Caballero, that most (Roman) Catholic of writers, lavishes on her; but in Madrid I never saw much evidence of popularity. When the last baby was born, I went to see the procession to the Atocha to present the little creature to the Virgin. The Prado was filled with the carriages of the grandees, each with their six or eight horses, with coloured plumes. Then came the foreign ministers, and all the great people, in full gala dress; and the Queen's riding-horses, magnificently caparisoned, and led by grooms clothed in gold tissue. Lastly, after all the Infantes and Infantas had passed in state carriages, came the great gilt-coach, containing the Queen and King, and the Asturian nurse, holding the baby. A few listless, uninterested-looking people were lounging on the Prado, nothing approaching to a crowd; but they took no sort of notice of the royal party, not even raising a hat as the Queen bowed from side to side. One heard a few half-jeering, half-growling remarks on the position of the King, and whispered hints that the right man was not in the right place, and that was all. I believe the Spanish people were never in the habit of cheering their sovereigns, but they appeared to me on this occasion to treat the most *piadosa* Isabel with positive rudeness.

Whatever the Queen may be, however, she never had a fair chance of being an honest woman, and she is at least as much sinned against as sinning. In her younger days, I believe, she was regularly encouraged and trained in all sorts of excesses by her mother, who was anxious to keep the power in her own hands by any means within reach.

The King looks like a little boy who has been very well whipped, and he is almost lost to sight behind his wife's portly figure. He is always spoken of with the greatest contempt, and is called "*Paquito*," the extreme diminutive of Francisco. He is a meagre, weak-looking little man, with a high treble voice, which makes him still more ridiculous.

They tell a story of him here, that at the time of the African war, O'Donnell was talking to the Queen about it, and she, becoming very enthusiastic, cried out, "*Ay, si yo fuere hombre, yo iria!*" "Ah, if I only were a man, I would go too."—"*Y yo tambien,*" "And so would I," squeaked the King.

I began this letter on Christmas Day, as you saw by the date, but am only finishing it to-day, the 28th, so I send you all my good wishes for the coming year with it.

January 18, 1864.

We had a pretty sharp frost since Christmas, during which the Estanque (I do not know if I can call it the ornamental water), in the Retiro, was frozen over, which is an extraordinary thing for Madrid. There were two or three people skating, and some hundreds looking on, muffled in their cloaks up to the eyes; but the ice was so covered with stones, which these bright creatures amused themselves by throwing on, that it was good for nothing. Since the frost broke up, we have had continual rain; the roads are mere rivers of mud, and everything looks dreary. I am beginning to tire of sitting in the house, with a view from my windows of a Chinese puzzle of roofs and dead walls, with a few chimney-pots by way of variety, and a flag, which waves proudly over a stable in the distance. There is a persistent drizzle going on, and a babel of dismal street-cries and discordant shouts of arrieros to their mules, which make you fancy you have strayed within hearing of Purgatory. In the house beneath us there are three disagreeable, fat girls, who are learning music, and from eight o'clock in the morning till seven o'clock at night they play the most dreary exercises—always the same, tumbling about on six notes, and picking themselves up again, all day long; and as one girl gets up another sits down, and after making a terrific scutter up to the top of the piano and down again, with a flop, in the shape of a great chord, all played wrong, she sinks hopelessly into the six-note exercise for the space of two or three hours; when number three takes her place, and goes over the same performance, scutter and all.

Every now and then they have a tertulia, and on

these occasions one of the young ladies plays a piece from 'Norma,' in which she is accompanied by a bass-viol; and though it is always the same piece, it has to be regularly rehearsed for several days before the eventful evening. So poor 'Norma,' for her sins, gets worried to death, and the violoncello groans, and bumps, and squeaks to the tune of her howlings, till we feel inclined to call down maledictions on the head of the man who first built houses in flats.

On one side we have a lady who sings operatic music, and you may imagine how pleasant it is, when I tell you that she shakes on each note as if she had palsy (as I think she has). This, with a running accompaniment of neuralgia in my own head, which laughs to scorn all remedies, makes it difficult to preserve patience, let alone cheerfulness.

January 20.

It is such a glorious morning, after all our miserable, dreary weather, that I can find no better vent for my spirits than writing to you. You should be in Madrid to know what sunshine is, for without it there is no place more hopelessly dismal; and then, when it does come back, it is such a rich, warm sun, with such a glorious, still, blue sky, and the air so deliciously balmy after the rain. These first days, after a spell of wet, are the perfection of weather, before the air becomes dry and scorching again, and the dust begins to fly. I have all the windows open, and have put the plants in the balcony to have the benefit of the air, and have half-closed the Venetian shutters, for the sun is very strong,—you cannot imagine how summery the room looks. My enemies downstairs have gone out for a walk, and left their poor piano to recover itself; and the palsied lady at the next door is also silent. Let us hope she has gone into the country for change of air.

Some of the Carnival festivities are already commencing, in the shape of masked balls, at some of the second-rate theatres; but the fun does not really begin until about the 7th. During the last week there are three balls given at the Theatre Royal, to which it is considered proper for ladies to go. The

Queen generally appears at some of them, though I do not know that that is any warrant of respectability.

Last night we went to the Opera, and heard Borghi Mamo in 'Sappho.' We found it utterly stupid, so we amused ourselves by laughing at the acting, which was very funny; especially when 'Sappho,' looking very much like a bundle of soiled clothes ready for the wash, tumbled herself off a manifestly pasteboard rock into the sea, and came out of it again to bow to the audience.

This last week the Queen has been making a pilgrimage round the churches, as she is expecting her confinement very soon; and one Virgin, who seems to be a kind of monthly nurse, and is very useful to ladies in these interesting circumstances, has been taken down from her altar, that her Majesty may the more easily implore her aid. There is an announcement in the papers to-day that any ladies who require her assistance may now go and ask for it. I do not know if this Vírgen del Cármen is supposed to be deaf, that it is necessary to bring her down from her throne. For the last four months we have had every particular of her Majesty's state announced in the paper from day to day, and when the happy event was first made public, which was some six months ago, all the public offices had a holiday, and Madrid was ordered to put on gala dress for three days. Now that the time is approaching, the Queen has her bed-room hung round and decorated with a leg of St. John, an arm of St. Luke, and sundry old teeth, bones, toe-nails, and locks of hair of the saints, so that she is certain to have a good time. Our little Princess managed pretty well without any of the saints' cast-off members,— but the circumstances are somewhat different.

February 3.

All Madrid seems to be going a little mad as the Carnival approaches. The shops are full of masks, and the streets of people; and the balls are beginning in earnest. We are going to have an open-carriage for the two principal days on the Prado.

February 4.

The modest sum we find they ask for a carriage during the Carnival is twelve dollars a day, and you must engage it for the whole four days; but we thought ten pounds rather much to pay for sitting four afternoons consecutively in the midst of Bedlam let loose, so I think we shall ride. I hope you can read my writing; but the fact is, it is such a deliciously beautiful morning that I must of necessity sit in the window—a French window, you know—opening on to the balcony, and sun myself like a cat, while I am waiting for Henry to come in to breakfast; and so it comes to pass that I am writing on my knee.

We have just come in from one of our mad performances on a favourite galloping ground outside the town, and, as it is twelve o'clock, I am as hungry as a hunter, and ready to devour anything but frogs, which Manuela gave us the other day for breakfast. They are considered a great delicacy here, and so are snails.

As we were coming down the Prado this morning, I was much amused by an old gentleman, who was exceedingly interested in watching me trot. He evidently thought there was some machinery about it, and at last he crossed to the middle of the road, and very carefully put on his spectacles, and watched my stirrup-foot, as well as he could see it, with the greatest interest; and as he stood so close that I almost grazed him in passing, I hope he knows now that it was all fair.

There is one great thing about fine weather here, that I can sit quite contentedly in the house, or rather in the balcony; whereas, if I were in England, I should want to be out in the fields, or under the trees, even if they were still bare of leaves. But here there are no trees and no fields, and you know the sun is only shining over miles of dust, and so do not wish to go out. If our dear little England had such a climate as this, we should not be able to imagine a heaven so beautiful, and should wish to be for ever "on this dull earth, where yet 'tis sweet to live." But England, with her grey skies and dull days, is worth ten thousand Spains, and one glimpse of her green woods and winding lanes, and all her wealth of wildflowers, is better than all the sunshine which pours unceasingly over this mangy landscape. But I must not be ungrateful. We have the mountains, and most beautiful they look now; every line softened by the soft white snow, which takes the delicate tints of the sunset, and dresses up the old hills in gala costume. Sometimes standing out in sharp relief against the deepest of deep blue skies; sometimes with soft, little, white clouds lingering round their summits and nestling tenderly in the hollows,—they stand in the changing light, and look so fairy-like that one forgets the dreary, drab plains that lie between. It seems so strange in a morning to find the sun almost too hot, and yet to have these snowy mountains apparently quite close.

February 16.

The Carnival is all over. Every one says it has been a very dull one; but, as I had never seen anything of the kind before, I was very much amused. It began on Sunday, the 11th, and the first we heard of it was a band, which came and serenaded us early in the morning. The players were all masked, and dressed as Zouaves; one of them came up into the drawing-room, on the strength of knowing Henry. These bands were going about all day, some of the players dressed in night-shirts reaching to below their knees, with white stockings and black boots, cats' faces, and enormous frilled nightcaps. In the afternoon the masks began to pass in great numbers on their way to the Prado, and by three o'clock there was a line of carriages extending the whole length of the Prado, going down one side and up the other. They are not allowed to break the line, and the whole centre of the road is reserved for the maskers and people on horseback.

Only men mask, as a rule, though there was one well-known carriage full of ladies, dressed in the old style, with powdered hair and patches, and little black masks over the eyes. They do not throw sweetmeats or flowers as in Italy, but carry them in boxes and present them to the ladies, mounting the carriages and chattering in feigned voices, like so many monkeys. Some favoured carriages will have four or five masks at once clinging on to it.

The favourite disguise seemed to be that of a lady, sometimes only with stays and petticoats on, sometimes in gorgeous ball costume, or a costly silk sweeping in the mud behind them. In this case the disguise is too good, for, being very small and effeminate-looking, you would not know the "pollos" from women, except that every now and then you will see one, with an enormous crinoline and sweeping train, jump up, astride, behind some friend who happens to be passing on horseback, and gallop down the Prado with his tarlatan and bouquets floating in the breeze behind him. Occasionally the horses also are masked; there was one with frilled white drawers on each leg, a sort of petticoat all round its body, and a black mask across its face. Every now and then one would come tearing past covered with bells, and some hideous devil or dragon seated on its back,— enough, you would think, to terrify any number of horses. Ours, however, behaved very well, only occasionally objecting when some frightful object approached a little too near, or touched them. Numbers of people go in the dress in which the penitents walk in the processions in Holy Week in Seville. They are completely enveloped in a long gown of black, or yellow, calico, with a tall extinguisher of the same on their heads, with two small holes for the eyes. They look horrible. There was one party of gentlemen, driving about in a little phaeton with six ponies, who were got up as wine-glasses and the driver as a bottle. Their legs formed the stem, and there was a wooden frame, covered with light grey calico, in the shape of the bowl of the glass, which completely covered the rest of their body, except that every now and then an arm would appear handing sweet-meats. Some adventurous spirits had fitted up an immense waggon to represent the roof of a house with attic windows, and they themselves, dressed as cats, went in and out miawling.

With all the riotous fun going on, the generality of the people struck me as taking their pleasure very sadly. I saw very few smiles, except on the faces of the children and the common people. But it must be rather dreary work in the carriages, as the masks remain, for the most part, in one portion of the Prado, between the Calle Alcalá and the Atocha, so that when the carriages have passed this part they have to go on to the Fuente Castellano, where there is no fun; and, as they can never get beyond a walk, the greater part of the day must be spent in creeping along the empty road to get round for a few moments to the favoured spot. In every way equestrians have the advantage, as they can go where they like, and turn whenever they choose. The masking on the Prado is kept up from Sunday morning till Wednesday evening, for the Spaniards do not appear to spend this day in sackcloth and ashes. During these four days the masks go about calling on their friends, especially in the evenings. The three great balls at the opera-house take place on Sunday, Tuesday, and—what seems strangest of all—on the following Sunday. They do not begin until about one o'clock in the morning, and last till daylight. I went to one with a party of friends, and was very much amused, the scene was so new and curious. The whole pit of the theatre is boarded over level with the stage, and you can have a private box to watch the fun. It is not the thing to dance, though there are always a number of couples performing in the centre of the room. Only ladies mask at these balls; gentlemen are not allowed to do so; and the correct dress is a black domino and mask, with only a rose or coloured ribbon as a distinguishing mark.

It is extraordinary how becoming these little black masks are; with their fall of lace over the lower part of the face, they make every woman look pretty; and as the Spanish women have all good eyes and most of them small, well-shaped chins, you would fancy you were wandering in a perfect wilderness of beauty. When the mask is off, the narrow, lined forehead and long cheeks of most of the faces spoil their beauty. There seem to be two distinctive styles of feature here: the short, plump face, which loves to paint Phillips, and which is much the prettiest type; and those with a singular length between the eyes and mouth; the foreheads are all low and narrow. Ford, you remember, says, "The beauty of the Spanish women is much exaggerated, at least as far as features and complexion are concerned. More loveliness is to be seen in one fine day in Regent Street than in a year in Spain." I certainly agree with him.

The principal amusement which the ladies find at these balls is attacking some gentleman whom they know, by sight at least, and chaffing him about matters which he fondly imagined to be a profound secret. The bystanders gather round and listen to the revelations of the tormentor, while the unfortunate victim can only try to penetrate the disguise of the mask and expose her in turn; he may use every means to this end short of raising the mask. Frequently the gentlemen pretend to be able to recognize the ladies by their hands, or try to catch a glimpse of the profile against the light. The maskers, of course, all speak in a feigned voice, and the effect in the crowded ballroom, where every one is talking at once, is extraordinary,—more like the sounds that greet you as you enter the monkey-house in the Zoological Gardens than anything else.

The Queen generally goes to one, at least, of the masked balls, but she and the ladies who attend her are now always dressed alike and in some distinctive costume, so that they are well known, and they keep together and only look on. Formerly she used to go really disguised and mix with the rest of the revellers, taking no inactive part in the fun. They tell a story of her going about once in the disguise of an officer, with a military favourite of the day, and getting into a dispute with a watchman, which ended by her striking him. The man arrested her, and she was obliged to discover herself to avoid being led off to the police-station.

I am told the ladies employ themselves for some time before the balls in raking up scandals and gathering information to be used against the victims of their attacks. Madrid is a wide field for this kind of thing, and Spanish ladies, even without the protection of a mask, are not in the least particular in what they say, so that I fancy it is pleasanter for an English lady to go while her knowledge of the language is somewhat imperfect, as mine is. Of the height to which scandal reaches in Madrid, it is enough to say that there is one lady who is celebrated here as being the only one among the higher rank about whom there is no "historiette scandaleuse."

THE GRACEFUL SPANISH DANCE, AS SEEN IN MADRID.

The movement and chatter in the ball-room give a much more lively idea of the people than the solemn faces of the occupants of the carriages on the Prado would lead one to expect, where the majority of the ladies look more as if they were going to a funeral than to the great fiesta of the year.

Talking of taking pleasure sadly, I do not know any more melancholy mirth than that you see here in the national dances, of which you hear so much in England. On the stage they are very pretty; the dancers in clean, handsome, "majo" dresses, look very well, and there is both grace and beauty in the figures, but the actual thing, as you see it on Sundays and feast days, in front of every little tavern outside of Madrid, can only be compared to the unhappy antics of those Savoyards in sheepskins and pointed hats, who twist slowly about, with spasmodic and painful efforts at liveliness, to the groan of a hurdy-gurdy, in the streets of London. Yet the people seem to like it. In every little open space outside the walls on a fiesta you will see a little crowd assembled, with a small clear place in the centre, where two or three couples are going through this dismal exercise, to the twanging of an invalid guitar. If there is anything graceful in the dance itself, it is difficult to discover it in the movements of the fat, sloppy servant girls, with bunchy petticoats and thick ankles, as they curvet in front of a sickly-looking boy-soldier, almost buried under his shako, or in the uniform of the celebrated cazadores here, which consists of a long brown coat, of coarse cloth, made the shape of a night-shirt, with a belt round the waist. If any dancer could look graceful under these circumstances, it would be marvellous. The people who stand round beat time by clapping their hands and stamping in a melancholy fashion. Altogether it is a parody on that "happy Continental life" we read of in books.

The Madrileño's idea, too, of a "day out" is peculiar. You see parties of six or eight, men and women, going out with their basket of provisions, and sitting down contentedly to eat them on the bare, brown ground, behind the bull-ring,—a few yards only from the Alcalá gate. Some, more adventurous, go in an omnibus as far as the first turnpike, about a mile from Madrid, and sit in the dust at the side of the road to eat their dinner "al fresco." If you can imagine picnicking in a brickfield, or on a plot laid out for building on, you will have some idea of the ground they choose for their excursion, but scarcely of the surrounding desolation. When the meal is ended, they get up one of these charming dances, and come home in the evening all slightly the worse for the " agua ardiente," which they have consumed during the day. This agua ardiente, is a mixture of a kind of gin and aniseed; I only know the smell, which is simply horrible. This is the gay Spanish life without varnish, and you may see any Sunday scores of these dusty picnics on any of the roads out of Madrid, but especially on those which are most barren and desolate-looking. The dances are a prolific source of quarrels, which frequently end in assassination. It is no uncommon thing for a man to stab his rival in the very midst of the dance, and then quietly make his way through the outer crowd and escape. These stabbing cases seem to be frightfully common. You never take up a paper without finding that a body has been found, "puñalado," somewhere outside the gates; and the assassin always seems to escape, as there are so many forms to be gone through before he can be even sought. In one case I heard of the alcalde of a village going out with a number of people to search for a murderer, which they did by all carrying lights and looking into the ditches and behind walls, like children playing at hide-and-seek.

March 20.

We have really decided on leaving for England this month, and intend going by Córdova, Seville, and Cadiz, to catch the Indian mail at Gibraltar. We have now finally fixed the 25th, having put it off from week to week for the last month. The rest of our party leave on the 22nd, to be in time for the processions in Holy Week in Seville. Judging from things Spanish in general, I imagine they will find them a delusion and a snare, and I am not sorry to miss them. Our beautiful weather has broken again, and it has been pouring for two days. I hope it will clear up in time to let us have one or two more rides to say good-bye to the mangy old plains, with their glorious background of mountains. Do not expect to hear from me again regularly after we leave Madrid, as we shall be moving about. We start on Good Friday, at half-past eight o'clock in the evening. I may not have time to write again, but will do so if possible.

LETTER VI.

Seville, *March* 29.

Here I am, all alone in the Fonda de Madrid, at Seville,—Henry having been obliged to go off on business to some distance this morning,—and the Emersons have just left for Cadiz, intending to stop on their way at Xeres to see the wine-vaults. So I have retired to my own room, which happens to be a very pleasant one, and shall employ myself in giving you some account of our journey so far, while I am waiting for Henry's return.

We left Madrid on Friday evening, as we intended (for a wonder!), and were escorted to the train by a numerous body of friends, so that we took quite an affecting farewell of poor old Madrid. At one o'clock we had to change carriages for Santa Cruz de Mudela, where we arrived about three o'clock A.M.; and after waiting an hour in the dismal, bare waiting-room, got packed into the diligence, in which we had secured the *coupé*, and started for Córdova. It was, of course, quite dark when we set out, and it would be vain to attempt to give you any idea of the road we had to jolt over. How on earth the lumbering old diligence, with its string of straggling mules, ever chanced to keep right end uppermost is more than I can conceive. It must have been under the care of that special Providence which is supposed to watch over drunken men and children; for there had been heavy rain for a fortnight, and when we were not in the water we were in ruts that were so deep as to take the wheels up to the axle-tree; and mules, at the best of times, have a fancy for spreading themselves all over the road, and taking a very zigzag course. When it became light, we were ascending the Sierra Morena, and the sun struggled out of the heavy clouds for a time, and made the scenery, which is very bold and rugged, look very fine. The pass is a very beautiful one, in some respects finer than those across the Pyrenees. When we began to descend the mountains, the day overclouded again, and we saw the road over which we were going to travel stretching before us in a hideously straight line, through a dismal, dripping landscape. To be sure, the country was green with the wheat, which appeared to be about a foot high, and covered with olive-trees; but these are but sad-looking shrubs at the best of times, and in the continuous drizzle looked miserable; and that terribly straight road, which looked as if it would never end, was almost enough to make one cut one's throat. Towards evening matters became worse; the rain fell in torrents, and the road became a river of mud full of deep holes. The mules could only go at a walk, while a man with a lantern and a long stick went before the leaders to guide them out of the worst pitfalls. To add to my misery, Henry was sleeping so comfortably, in spite of the jolts, that I was a prey to the direst envy as I saw him quietly unconscious of the way he was being banged about,—now with his head against the roof, now almost pitching out of the window, and then, again, tumbling on to the top of me,—I do believe he could sleep on the top of a pike. Instead of a twelve-hours' drive, as we had fondly anticipated, we had twenty, and did not arrive in Córdova till twelve o'clock, and then were taken to the railway-station, which is about a mile and a half from the town, and had to wait an hour there while the train to Seville was dispatched; so that we were rather glad to find ourselves at the Fonda Rizzi, and get some dinner, at two o'clock on Sunday morning, having travelled without stopping from Friday evening; and for twenty hours I had never stirred out of the *coupé* of the diligence, so I think I am a pretty good traveller.

From twelve o'clock on the Thursday morning before we left Madrid no carriages had been allowed to go out, the bells of the churches were silent, and no music in any of the services; the windows of the churches were darkened, and the altars illuminated. The whole of Thursday is taken up by the faithful in visiting as many churches as possible; the Queen sets the example, going on foot to the seven nearest to her. On Saturday morning, at ten o'clock, suddenly all the bells begin to ring, cannons are fired, and the Gloria is sung, in honour of the resurrection; I cannot understand why they make it a day earlier than we do. We happened to be changing mules in a little village on the mountains just as the clock struck ten, and in an instant there was a clamour that would have terrified anything but diligence mules,—bells clashed, guns fired, and squibs and crackers were let off on all sides. During these two days the Spaniards tell you that God is dead, and that therefore you ought not to sin, since you are on your honour.

Córdova is a curious old town, though showing no trace of the immense extent of ground it formerly covered. We spent our time there in wandering about the curious old cathedral, with its forest of marble pillars and Moorish arches, or sitting in the sun listening to the rush of the Guadalquivir, now a fine rolling river after the rains. The streets are so narrow that no sort of vehicle, except perhaps a wheelbarrow, can pass down them. Going to the station, we had to walk from the hotel to the little square from which the omnibus starts, and the street it goes through is so tight a fit for it that the walls of the houses on each side are all dinged and chipped, and a man stands behind the driver's seat for the express purpose of guiding it through, with his hand pushing against, now one side, and now the other. If any one happens to be in the street, he must turn back, or squeeze himself into a doorway until the omnibus passes.

The cathedral is built on the site of a mosque, which is said to have been a triumph of Moorish art; one portion of it still remains in what is called the Moorish Chapel. The very beautiful marble pillars, with their curious low arches, were also retained. What I enjoyed most of all was sitting under the orange-trees in the patio, and listening to the pealing of the organ. It was Easter Day, but, considering the length of our journey from Madrid, you may easily imagine we were not up in time to hear Mass in the morning. We were most comfortably lodged in the Fonda Rizzi, and shall for ever feel grateful for the excellent dinner we got there, at two o'clock in the morning, on our arrival. The houses are all built round a patio, as in Madrid, only that here the patios are filled with flowers, and have a fountain in the centre. Marble is so common in Spain that all the floors and pillars are made of it, and look very rich and cool.

It is only a four hours' journey from Córdova to Seville, and we arrived here on Sunday evening, in time for a late dinner. We found our friends, as we expected, highly disgusted with the processions; there was nothing to be seen worth the trouble and annoyance of waiting in the crowd for. The first thing we did on Monday morning was to go to the cathedral, which is now all hung with crimson velvet and tapestry, in consequence of its being Easter Week. There is a huge monument, as they call it, a structure of imitation marble and gold, which reaches up to the roof of the cathedral, placed just over Columbus's tomb, so that we could not see it. The cathedral is a glorious building. Oh! how we enjoyed wandering about among the arches, over the cool, marble floor, with the sunlight streaming in through the stained windows; and the organ swelling and pealing, now in tumultuous, passionate sounds, now dying off in sweet, low tones; for being Easter Week there was always some service going on. The carvings in the choir are most exquisite, and so are the two great organs which form the sides of it, and reach up to the roof. Or, strolling quietly up the Giralda, the old Moorish tower, which now serves as a clock-tower to the cathedral, we would lean against the window, looking down upon the patio of oranges below, and listen to the organ from there. We could scarcely make up our minds to leave the cathedral. The Giralda is ascended by inclined planes instead of steps, so that you could ride up it; it is not nearly so fatiguing, therefore, as an ordinary tower. From the top, as you stand just beneath the great bells, there is a splendid view of Seville, with her gardens and stately river, her numerous churches, and the Moorish Alcáza, which is close by. This cathedral is also built on the site of the ancient mosque. They show you in one of the chapels the tomb of San Fernando; I believe through a glass window in the outer coffin, the foot of this conqueror of the Moors is to be seen uncorrupted, but we were not curious enough to wish to see it; indeed, all my sympathies go with the Moors, and not with the Spaniards. It is impossible to feel otherwise when you see the glorious traces they left behind them. Everywhere they passed, there are splendid palaces, churches, and towns; everywhere a smiling country, with rich cultivated fields, and every natural resource utilized. Valencia owes all its beauty and wealth to them; for the irrigation works, which have turned the whole province into a garden, are theirs. Their towns were built on the most splendid sites that could be chosen, and their private houses were like palaces. And what have the Spaniards done? Cut down the trees, and burnt them for firewood; and made the country an arid waste. On the ruins of the Moorish cities they have erected their mud hovels, and their houses* tied together with string;

---

* This is no figure of speech, for the houses are literally tied together with string, as you may see in any building in course of erection in Madrid. There is a framework of wooden beams, fastened together with what appears to be ordinary twine of a tolerable thickness; inside this the bricks are set, about two deep, and the outside is afterwards stuccoed. This must add considerably to the cost of building, because all kinds of wood and in place of the industry, which made the country rich and beautiful, there is now a crowd of effeminate idlers lounging for ever in the sun, and smoking paper-cigars. Ford tells us that Madrid was originally chosen as a royal residence, on account of the vast forests that surrounded it. Where are they now? Gone to cook the puchero of these wretched people, who cut their own throats, and then wonder that they are like to die.

We spent many hours in the Alcázar, which has been carefully restored and is kept in good order. You can form a very good idea of it from the Alhambra Court in the Crystal Palace; but it is the extent, and the variety of the intricate and beautiful decorations, the cool, dark rooms, with their murmuring fountains, and lofty, arched ceilings, which give the charm and, in this hot climate,

are so expensive in Madrid. Although coal is from £4. 10s. to £5 a ton, it is cheaper firing than wood.

The mud hovels which are to be seen outside the city are built by means of a wooden mould, consisting of two parallel boards, about eighteen inches apart, which is placed on the ground, and filled with layers of mud, each layer being well trodden down by the feet of the workmen. When the mould is full, it is moved on, and another portion of the wall commenced, leaving the first to harden in the sun.

form a Paradise. The gardens, too, are beautiful, and full of rare flowers. Some of the fountains are completely bordered with a luxuriant growth of maiden-hair fern; seeing me admire it, one of the gardeners gathered me a large handful, telling me it was used medicinally; he did not seem to think it at all beautiful, and was astonished that I cared to have it. From the garden you descend a few steps to the baths of Doña Maria de Padilla, and deliciously luxurious they must have been. Some of the paths in the garden are tiled, and water is laid on below; so that by turning a screw, little jets of water spring up from innumerable holes in the pavement and form an archway of miniature fountains; this is a contrivance for keeping the tiles always cool and clean. The gardeners, of course, always warn you off the walk before they turn on the water, or the consequences might be unpleasant.

At the door of the Hall of Ambassadors they show you the stain of the blood of the unfortunate son of Alonso XI. and Doña Leonor de Guzman, who was murdered here by order of his brother,

Pedro the Cruel. The story goes that Don Fedrique was pacing this hall, pondering on the strange reception he had met with from Maria Padilla, whom he had just left, and whose rooms were on the other side of the Patio de las Doncellas; for she knew of the intentions of the King, and neither dared to warn him, nor could she dissemble, as Don Pedro had done, congratulating him on the victories he had just gained in Murcia. It was while thinking thus that the creatures of the King entered and attacked him from behind. He tried to defend himself, but the hilt of his sword became fixed in the scabbard and he could not withdraw it. He fled through the beautiful Patio de las Muñecas towards the Hall of Ambassadors, at the door of which he fell; while, it is said, his brother quietly watched the murder from behind a grating in the Queen's apartments, and even gave his own dagger to a valet to give a final blow at the still-palpitating heart of the Master of Santiago.

Yesterday we spent at the Museo. In the Salon de Murillo are no less than twenty-four of the works of this great artist. Some of the most beautiful of his paintings are here. There is a story about one of them,—the "Vírgen de la Servilléta,"—that when Murillo was painting in some monastery, the monk who brought him his dinner asked him to paint him a picture of the Virgin for his cell. Murillo made no answer; but when the monk took away the remains of the dinner he missed the napkin on which it was served. The following day Murillo presented him with the napkin with this head of the Virgin painted on it. The closest inspection, however, fails to show any difference in the texture of the canvas of this picture from any other.

Seville is so full of places of interest that one scarcely knows where to begin to speak of them. There is a beautiful Moorish palace belonging to the Duke of Medina Celi, called the Casa de Pilatos, because it is supposed to be built on the exact model of Pilate's house. I can only say I admire Pilate's taste a great deal more than that of the Duke of Medina Celi, and wonder how the latter can live in that ginger-bread palace of his in Madrid when he has such a place as this to come to. The caretaker, however, told us the family were never there; and, indeed, the house is not furnished. It is in the same style as the Alcázar, but, of course, smaller. Seville appears to be fifty years in advance of Madrid, and is in every way pleasanter; the houses are very pretty and look very homelike with their handsome patios full of flowers,—each with its cool, dripping fountain and marble pavement. These patios are covered with an awning in the hot weather, and the people seem to live in them. In the evenings you hear voices and laughter, and catch glimpses of merry parties through the handsome iron gates which close most of them. We have a nice patio full of arum-lilies and roses in our hotel, and a colonnade running all round it, to which every one adjourns after dinner for coffee. The Andaluz costume is very pretty; the men wear knee-breeches of black cloth with a row of silver buttons at the side, terminating in a handsome silk tassel at the knee; white stockings; and leather gaiters, beautifully embroidered, and left open at the calf; a very fine linen shirt, elaborately embroidered, with gold studs; a crimson silk *faja*; and over all, a jacket of fine black cloth, trimmed with a thick black-silk cord and buttons, and embroidered on the elbows

ANDALUSIAN DRESS.

and down the back; a black-felt hat with a turned-up rim, covered with velvet and ornamented by the usual black-silk tufts. These hats are almost the shape of the "pork-pies," but have a much broader brim. The jacket is sometimes of a black fur which looks like Astracan. The woman's dress, I believe, is a short skirt trimmed with rows of silk bob-fringe; a velvet waistcoat, like a man's, with silver buttons down the edge; a crimson *faja;* a jacket handsomely braided; and a small bull-fighter's hat. But I imagine this dress has almost, if not quite, disappeared now amongst the women, —at least we never saw it, though the men of the farmer class all wear the " traje Andaluz." We spent one afternoon on the Alameda,—the fashionable promenade of Seville. It follows the course of the river, and is beautifully planted with trees. The scene was very Spanish, for French bonnets have not yet invaded Seville and put to flight the graceful vela.

We saw the Comte de Paris riding with his young *fiancée;* she looked pretty, and not at all of a Spanish style. The Duke and Duchess of Montpensier live in the palace of San Telmo, a great staring-looking building, close to the Alameda, but surrounded by pretty gardens. They used to have the Alcázar, and in one of the principal rooms a stone has been let into the Moorish mosaic-work to record the interesting fact that, close to that spot, the Infanta Isabel, daughter of the Duke and Duchess, first saw the light. On the opposite side of the river to San Telmo is the Torre del Oro, an old Moorish tower, and there also lies the Triana, the gipsies' quarter, with which Phillips's pictures have made every one familiar. We have had lovely weather ever since we have been in Seville; it is a little hot, but there is plenty of shade, and it is so delightful to have trees and flowers about you.

I cannot say I admire the manners of the Spaniards whom we meet in travelling. The ladies behave at table in the way we are accustomed to imagine that washerwomen do, using their knives in preference to forks, and their fingers in preference to knives, snuffling, and picking their teeth, while they lean with both elbows on the table, and turn round occasionally to spit on the floor. We have a marquis and his wife and daughter opposite to us at table, who certainly make me stare sometimes. The ladies come down to breakfast, with their faces unwashed and their hair just as they have slept in it, in dirty dressing-gowns, and with greasy silk handkerchiefs round their necks, on which may be seen many an ancient tide-mark. But in the afternoon they come out in gorgeous costumes, wash the front of their faces, and have their hair done by a hair-dresser in marvellous horns and rolls. This custom of not dressing till the afternoon seems almost universal in Spain, and there is nothing the Spaniards express so much astonishment at as the morning toilets of Englishwomen. It seems as little remarkable for a Spanish lady to spit as for her to eat her dinner. Riding down the Prado one day in Madrid, I saw a very elegantly-dressed and pretty woman interrupt what she was saying to a gentleman who was with her, to lean forward and spit out of the window of her brougham. One excuse I must make for them, that the air of Madrid, being so rarefied rom the height of its situation, gives one a constant cold in the head, with its consequent thickening in the throat; but still, they have pocket-handkerchiefs.

Another thing about the Spanish women is that they talk so loud, always at the top of their voices, leaning on the table and digging at their teeth meanwhile. However, I need not say much when I heard one of my countrywomen call out in a loud voice to a friend at the other side of the dinner-table, when asked about some hotel, "Oh, it is jolly, and the grub is first-rate."

LETTER VII.

GIBRALTAR, *April* 9.

WE left Seville with regret, for we had enjoyed our visit there very much; but as we found it quite impossible to obtain any information about the Indian steamer from Gibraltar, or even the Spanish one from Cadiz, we were obliged to take our chance. On our arrival at Cadiz, we found no steamer would be going for three days, and even then we could not find out how long we should have to wait here for a boat home. Cadiz is a clean, rather pretty little place; but I think I should go mad if I had to live there. It is built on a narrow strip of land, which is an island at high-water; and the little neck that joins it to the mainland is strongly fortified, so that you feel exactly as if you were in prison. You have no enjoyment of the sea either, for on every side are fortifications, so that you can only see it over a wall. The streets are very narrow, so that you can comfortably talk to your neighbours across them, and almost shake hands. The houses are handsome, and many of them have solid mahogany doors, remnants of the days of Spain's glory. We had soon exhausted all the sights of Cadiz, and should have found it intolerably dull only that the weather was so lovely. We took a carriage and drove on to the mainland for some distance, and spent an hour or two by the seashore, where I found some very beautiful little shells,—glad to be free from the everlasting sentries and the interminable fortifications. Speaking of these, however, I should think they would not be difficult to demolish, for not a single gun seemed to be fit for use: the carriages had rotted away from under many of them, and they were lying half-buried in drifted sand. We were glad when the morning arrived for our departure. The steamer started at half-past five on Sunday morning, so we had to be up betimes. I shall never forget the sunrise. It was dusk when I got up, but before I was dressed the sky was all one rosy light; and as we left the pier and pulled off to the steamer, which was moored in the bay, the sun rose majestically from the sea. Cadiz looked splendid in the morning light, with its long façade of handsome white buildings skirting the bay,—much better than it does on a closer inspection.

We had a delicious trip to Gibraltar, keeping close in to the shore all the way, almost within a stone's throw, and crossing Trafalgar Bay, which we looked at with much interest, trying to realize to ourselves that we really saw the famous battle-ground in the glassy waters that we were steaming through. About one o'clock, I think, we passed the Straits, and saw the snowy peaks of the African mountains on one side, while Spain lay burning beneath the blazing sun on the other. The first sight of Gibraltar is very striking,—the rock stands out like a great lion, looking seaward,—all the more so that the land immediately behind is very flat.

We went to Algesiras first, where, it is said, the Spanish governor of Gibraltar lives during the "temporary occupation of the English." Being Sunday, the captain could not land his cargo, and would not leave without doing so, and we seemed likely to spend the afternoon frizzling in the sun, not knowing at what moment the steamer from Alexandria might come in, for we had heard on board that she was overdue.

However, at last, the captain came to some arrangement with the officials, who had come off from the shore, and we steamed across the bay and landed about four o'clock. A word about this Spanish captain. He was so much afraid of any one thinking that he ever demeaned himself by work, that he kept his nails half an inch longer than his fingers, and pointed like a bird's claws, —he looked like a cannibal!

Henry had secured rooms at the King's Arms. We had been recommended to go there in preference to the Club House Hotel, as the attendance and food were said to be better. It is rather a poor-looking place outside, but our first dinner

certainly justified all that we had heard. In the
evening we went up to the parade-ground, which
is at some height above the town, and is surrounded by woods and gardens, kept in most
exquisite order. Here we sat, under the trees,
looking across the bay, with its little fleet of vessels riding at anchor, until it was dark, and even
long after,—for it was eleven o'clock before we
returned to the hotel. We were set at rest about
the steamer the next day, for a telegram arrived
saying that there had been some accident at Alexandria, and it would not be in for three days.
We were not sorry to have this time to make acquaintance with the Rock, though we should have
liked to have been able to run over to Tangiers
before starting for England. The windows of our
sitting-room look upon the market-place, where
every nation under the sun seems to have sent a
representative: there is the cunning Greek, and
the solemn Turk; the ragged, dirty Arab, wrapped
in his burnous, and the stately, handsome Moor,
looking fifty times better than the little starveling
Spaniard who minces beside him in patent-leather

boots. Spaniards seem fond of Gibraltar; you see them everywhere, and in every variety of costume; and I noticed, in other parts of Spain, that they were always proud to be able to boast that they had been born on the Rock.

Yesterday we started on horseback to see the galleries, and go up to the signal-station. It was a lovely morning, and we mounted the steep road that winds up the face of the rock, in the hope of a splendid view from the summit. Looking at it from the sea, Gibraltar scarcely seems to be fortified at all, except just above the sea-line, unless the soldiers happen to be practising some of the batteries, which they do every morning, and then the flash and puff of white smoke tells of them hidden all over the rock. The town lies in a snug little hollow, on the west side; and, after passing it, you begin the ascent at once, coming upon numbers of batteries, completely masked by luxuriant banks of shrubs and flowers. Each gun is ready, with its store of powder and balls by its side, to be fired at a moment's notice. We could not help comparing them with the dismantled old lumber at

Cadiz, which must be perfectly useless in case of a sudden attack. You come at last to the galleries, which are tunneled out of the rock, and are, of course, almost dark,—the little light there is coming in through the small holes, which are only just large enough to allow the muzzle of the gun to be pointed down on the bay.

My horse, being white, was the only one that was visible; but the creatures seemed quite contented to grope along in the dark, and we trusted entirely to them. Every now and then we emerged into the dazzling sunshine again, blinking like owls, and found the grey old rock gay with innumerable wild-flowers. I noticed quantities of wild iris, and that striped blue agapanthus we used to have in our greenhouse. At last we had to leave our horses with our guide, and proceed on foot,—the soldier, who was our cicerone, promising us a splendid view from St. George's Hall, a large cave, with an opening looking towards Spain, over the neutral ground. Nelson is said to have dined here when at Gibraltar. But when, after passing a gallery rather longer and darker than usual, we emerged into the high, vaulted chamber, with its battery of guns, and its opening landward, we seemed to have passed into another world. Nothing was to be seen but a thick, white vapour, pouring in through the aperture, and on looking down on what ought to be the view, there was nothing but huge masses of cloud, looking as substantial as cotton-wool. We felt exactly like two cherubim in our native element. "It is the levante," said our guide; "you can never tell when it will come on this way all of a sudden."

We waited for some time to see if it would clear off, but it only did so for an instant, giving us a glimpse of the water, and the coast lying far below, like a fairy land, and closing over again immediately. There was nothing to be done; the signal-station was hopeless for that day, so we returned to our horses, which we found standing damp and dismal, with heads and tails drooping. We mounted, and rode carefully down again, for we could not see more than a couple of yards before us; but before we reached the town we were in sunshine again. We were very damp, and altogether thought it would not be very pleasant to be cherubim. We went across the neutral ground for a gallop to dry ourselves, and saw our friends, the clouds, still shrouding the whole summit of the old lion in their moist embrace. We passed the racecourse, and the cemetery, and the English and Spanish sentries, showing the boundary of the two nations' dominion. We were in Spain again, as we could easily perceive by the slovenly, careless soldier, lounging against his dirty sentry-box, smoking his paper cigar, while our own smart red-coat was pacing steadily on his beat within a few yards of him. It seemed like a dream; we had been in England a moment before, hearing our own language, and seeing our own countrymen on every side. Now we were passing a squalid Spanish village, with all its dirt and discomfort. Gibraltar is a place to make English people feel very proud, but one would think it must be a terrible thorn in Spain's side; and I could not help thinking that, if I had been the Spanish staff officer I saw strutting down the street, on our return, with his plume of white feathers, I would have kept away from the place, or entered it in plain clothes. The next day being clear, we started for the signal-station on foot, and spent a glorious day, climbing the rock at our leisure, and sitting to rest, while we enjoyed the view across the bay to the Spanish coast on the other side. We saw an officer's funeral creeping slowly along below us towards the cemetery, and could hear the beautiful 'Dead March in Saul,' though the figures of the men following the procession looked so small as to be scarcely distinguishable. The whole rock was covered with wild-flowers, iris, saxifrage, and a beautiful little crimson vetch, with two damask brown leaves, and numbers of others; indeed, the variety was so great that, though I only gathered one or two of each different flower, my bouquet was too large to hold comfortably before I reached the top.

At the signal-station we were very glad to find some bitter ale, for we were both hot and thirsty, and then we enjoyed the splendid view,—the blue Mediterranean stretching away to the African coast; the little bay below us, with its crowd of vessels; and Spain lying behind us, with her arid fields and blazing sands: for from the summit of the rock you have, of course, an uninterrupted view on every side. The eastern side of the rock is very steep; it appears to descend perpendicularly to the water's edge at one point, and from the parapet of the signal-station we threw a stone straight down into the sea, though it was lost to sight long before it reached it.

I have been tiring my eyes, and breaking my neck, all the time I have been in Gibraltar, looking for monkeys, which you know are found on the rock. The signal-man told me he had seen three the day before just below where we stood, and even excited my hopes by saying he thought he saw two at that moment basking in the sun, a mother and child; but, on fetching his glass, they proved to be a large grey stone and a little grey stone, side by side.

All day long the porpoises have been leaping about in the bay, cutting through the water in sharp lines, and throwing off the spray in glittering showers. At night they look so beautiful when the sea is phosphorescent.

LETTER VIII.

On board the 'Palestine,' *April* 12, 1864.

I shall write this letter as a kind of journal, by way of passing the time on shipboard, and shall post it at Southampton, where we shall stay a few days with our friends the Elliotts before going on to London.

We were four days at Gibraltar, and enjoyed it very much. We had glorious weather, and lived out-of-doors, spending our mornings in lounging about in the beautiful woods which skirt the Alameda, and the afternoons in making riding or walking expeditions to the eastern side of the rock, or into Spain. In the evenings the band plays on the parade-ground, and we chose a quiet spot in the woods, away from the crowd, and listened to it from the distance. Later on, the band of the 'Racoon,' which was anchored in the bay, would begin, and we always remained out enjoying the cool evening air and listening to the music coming, softened, across the water, and did not return to the hotel until ten or eleven o'clock.

There is a pretty little old cemetery nestling in the hollow of a huge rock, full of flowers,—arum-lilies, and geraniums,—but in all parts of the rock, among the plantations which cover the lower part of it, you come upon single graves, with their simple headstones carefully preserved and their flowers well tended. They were chiefly tombs of officers, who had been buried, I suppose, before any regular cemetery was laid out.

Some of the houses scattered about the rock are perfect little paradises, with their hedges of tall geranium separating them from the road, and their beautiful view over the sea.

At eight o'clock every evening there is a sudden flash and boom from the signal-station; that is the evening gun, and after it is fired no one is allowed to enter or leave the rock by sea or land. This regulation proved rather a nuisance to us, for the 'Palestine' not being telegraphed during the day, she was expected to come in during the night, in which case she would merely take the mails, which were to be sent out to the coal-hulk, and go on without waiting for passengers; so we were obliged to go to the coal-hulk too, to wait for her. We had, moreover, to start an hour sooner than we need have done, to allow time for our boatmen to get home again before gun-fire, or they would have had to remain in the bay all night. The mails were not going on board till eleven, and at first we were told we might go with them, but at the last moment it turned out that one of the princes of the French family of Bourbons was going, with his attendants, and the boat would be required for him; so we set out at seven o'clock, and mounted the dirtiest old hulk you can imagine, with coals tumbling about in every direction. The man in charge professed great regret that he had not known there was a lady coming, or he would have had the deck cleaned up a little. However, he spread a tarpaulin, somewhat less coaly than the boards, and by the help of our own rugs and a couple of camp-stools, which we found on board, we made the best of our situation. We had a splendid sunset, and enjoyed listening to the band of the 'Racoon;' but by-and-by it became unmistakably chilly, and we were sick of watching for the lights of the steamer to come round the point of the rock. About ten o'clock the captain came to say he did not think the vessel would be in before morning, and to offer me his cabin, which we were very thankful to accept. It was very small, but there were two sofas in it, and, what was still better, two clean pillows; so we rolled ourselves in our rugs and went to sleep. At eleven we heard the French prince come on board, and I did not grudge him his mail-boat, as he had to remain in the coaly outer-cabin, with hard benches and no pillows. After all, the 'Palestine' did not come in till after gun-fire in the morning, so we might as well have slept comfortably at the hotel. We scrambled on board as soon as she came to anchor, feeling and looking very like coal-heavers, and immediately retired to our cabins to wash off the grime before appearing at breakfast. While in my cabin, I heard the other passengers talking in the saloon. Some of them had been on shore, and were describing what they had seen; but what struck me at once was the sweet voices of the Englishwomen. How gently and quietly they all spoke, after the Spanish screech! And what ladies they all seemed afterwards, when we met them at table!—no more picking and sucking of teeth; no more unwashed faces, and greasy neckerchiefs; no more knife or finger exercise. And what giants they all looked! In Spain, I had come to think myself quite tall; and now I had again sunk to my original insignificant dimensions.

LETTER IX.

SOUTHAMPTON, *April* 17.

OUR five days' voyage was delightful. We found an old friend on board, and got on capitally. We had a beautiful passage;—of course a little tossing in the Bay of Biscay, but otherwise it was as calm as a duck-pond.

We had not many passengers on board: I think about sixty-eight generally sat down to dinner; they were chiefly invalids. There was one man who looked more dead than alive, and made me think of John the Baptist with his head stuck on again; he was always talking about his complaints at meal-times, and was quite sufficiently suggestive without. Then there was a sickly young fellow, with a large, overhanging forehead, who could not have been long in India; and an old man with a wrinkled face, but kindly expression, broken down before his time; next to him sat a missionary, with lank hair and large feet, and flapping, melancholy-looking clothes, who was always arguing with John the Baptist; and the usual number of officers and their wives, with tribes of children with bleached faces and straw-coloured hair.

One poor little baby, there was, dressed in deep mourning, looking the picture of ill-health, with large, melancholy eyes, whom an ayah was bringing home. It had just lost its mother, poor little thing, and seemed to know it, so sad was the expression of its baby face.

The first day I was on board I laughed at the number of meals the passengers ate, and the eager way they rushed off when the bell rang, as if they had not been fed for a week. The second day I went down to see them eat, and the third day I ate as much myself;—it is all you can do on shipboard.

On the evening of the fourth day we had a grand dinner, and a great deal of speechifying, and the gentlemen remained on deck for a long time after the lights were out, singing glees. At daybreak the next morning I awoke, and found we were passing the Needles. On going on deck I found all the Indian passengers in a great state of excitement as they neared home. The ladies came out in their best clothes to go ashore. Some Cockney-minded gentlemen made their appearance with a fresh white turban twisted round their hats, though they had not needed them at all, or worn them, since they had left Gibraltar: but it was necessary to let every one know where they had come from, just as you see Brown, Jones, and Robinson clutching their alpenstocks with ferociously-brave looks, on board the Calais boat. Even the French Comte went below, and shortly after reappeared with a small black moustache, instead of the little lemon-coloured one he had worn during the voyage.

As we neared the quay the excitement became intense; every one crowded to the side of the boat to try and distinguish friends among the crowds waiting on shore. There was one thoroughly English-looking young fellow on board, whom we christened "Jack," because the name seemed to suit him and we did not know his own. He had been up on the paddle-box for some time with a telescope; suddenly he came flying down as if he were going to break his neck, and, seizing the first person he met,—which happened to be the fat, good-natured purser,—began shaking his hand violently, while he cried, "I say, old fellow, there's the governor on the quay." "All right," said the purser, "I am glad to hear it." Away rushed Jack to have another look, shaking hands with every one he met on the way. When we actually touched, and people were allowed to come on deck, the scene was very amusing; and as we were such recent travellers and had no one to meet us, and but very little luggage, we had nothing to do but to watch our neighbours. I looked out especially for the "governor," and saw Jack take forcible possession of a stiff and rather sombre-looking old clergyman, whom he dragged about with him, talking vociferously and shaking hands in the wildest way with every one. One would have thought we were the dearest friends he had by the way he wrung ours at parting. The last I saw of his good-humoured face was as we were sitting in the railway carriage waiting for our train to start. Another train passed us going out of the station, and from out of a first-class window appeared Jack's head and arm, waving his cap as long as he was in sight.

The pale young man with the large forehead had got a delicate-looking widowed mother, and young sister, who were trying to make him put a comforter round his neck and wrap himself in an overcoat. Another of the passengers had found his son, whom he had sent home almost an infant, a tall, strapping young fellow with a beard and moustache, and kept looking at him as if trying to identify him with the cherub-face he remembered. The old man with the wrinkles was pacing the quay with a pretty fair-haired daughter hanging on to his arm with both hands, and looking up into his seamed old face as if he were a god at least. I don't know what had become of John the Baptist; he had disappeared, but I felt sure he was telling some one the particulars of his illness, and I was glad it was not me. The missionary with the flapping clothes had also gone to talk about his converts to some other audience; but the melancholy little motherless baby was fetched away by a severe old man, who looked as if he had swallowed the poker and it had disagreed with him. I hoped it would die, poor little thing, as I saw the cold, dreary-looking old man, with his black satin stock half a yard high and his sour face, march off with it without one word of tenderness or welcome.

How beautiful England looks, with the deep meadows and fresh green hedges, the neat little homesteads and blooming gardens! Only the sun seems to throw no shadow; in fact, it scarcely seems to have pierced the clouds yet. It will come out by-and-by;—I look up: there are no clouds, only a white veil all over the sky, which makes the blue look grey. Will it come out by-and-by? or is this the English sun? Every one I meet says, "Is it not a glorious day? We have had sunshine like this for a fortnight." Never mind; if there were no sun at all, it would be better than Spain.

LETTER X.

MADRID, *August* 23, 1865.

I WROTE a line this morning just to say we had arrived, but, as the early post goes out at half-past two, I had not time to do more.

We had a very pleasant journey, except the portion between Calais and Paris, where we were almost smothered with dust, and consequently arrived at the Hôtel Choiseul only fit to be touched with tongs. We left Paris on Sunday evening, and were fortunate enough to have the carriage to ourselves as far as Bordeaux; and from thence we had a *coupé*. Rain had fallen during the night and early morning, so there was no dust, and we arrived at Bayonne at half-past twelve o'clock on Monday, quite fresh, and ready for a drive to Biarritz. We found Bayonne looking prettier and cleaner than ever. I cannot imagine why it is not a much greater favourite with English people than it appears to be, for it is a picturesque little place, having moreover a good deal of historical interest, and combines all that is needful for fine scenery,—mountains in abundance, a fine river, the sea, and woods and cultivated land on all sides, so that it has none of the barrenness of a seaside place. I like it very much, and fancy it would make a charming resting-place from whence to make excursions into the Pyrenees.

After lunching at the St. Étienne, our old hotel, which I liked much in our last visit to Bayonne, we drove to Biarritz, through the pine-wood, and returned in the evening by the old diligence road, which is almost a continuous avenue of fine trees. Before going to call on the A———s, who are staying at Biarritz, we walked about on the rocks for an hour, and amused ourselves by watching the bathers floundering about in the clear water. In a little bay, called Vieux Port, which is almost enclosed by high cliffs, is the fashionable bathing-place. There is a long row of houses on the shore for the use of the bathers, who, having put on the very elegant costume which is now worn in the water, go down composedly through the crowd of spectators to take their bath. In front of the bathing-houses is a band-stand, but there were no musicians there when we saw it. Ladies and gentlemen all bathe together, and the difference in their costume is so slight as to be scarcely distinguishable in the water.

We sat on the top of one of the cliffs, which jut out into the sea on each side of the little bay, so that we were exactly over the swimming-ground; and a very funny scene it presented, for the water was so clear that all the bathers were visible as they kicked about in different directions, looking like so many large parti-coloured frogs. Occasionally some frog, unaccustomed to swimming, would come to grief, and splutter about in a desperate manner, having recourse at last to the bladders, which the bathing-men keep ready for those who require them. Others would get on to the rocks, which stand up here and there out of the water, and quietly sun themselves, taking a header in again whenever the fancy took them. One man, who had been sitting thus for a long time, took a sudden fancy for a dive, and we watched him go right down through the clear water, and come up again against the broad back of an unsuspecting old gentleman, in a dress of yellow and red stripes, who was quietly disporting himself at a little distance. The poor old man was highly indignant, and gesticulated frantically, when he had recovered sufficiently to do so, for he was pitched head over heels in the water by the blow, and was some time in righting himself. Some of the ladies swam very well, though they did not seem to be able to go very fast. They come down to the water's edge in a waterproof cloak over their bathing-dress, and leave it with an attendant, to be put on again as soon as they come out; and as they have to walk through all the promenaders, and past the band, it is not an unnecessary precaution. On the whole, we came to the conclusion that man was not meant to be a swimming animal, for he certainly does not look dignified in the water. We could not help thinking of Carlyle's (or rather Shakespeare's) "forked carrots with fantastically-carved heads."

From the A——s I received a dreadful account of the custom-house officers in Madrid, who, they said, were stricter and more vexatious than ever. I did not, however, find them very terrible; they merely looked at my portmanteau, and let me off without charging duty for anything. I put the only thing that was at all doubtful at the top, so that they might see it at once, and I am always very polite in giving them my keys and showing them how to open all the different divisions of my trunk. Either that, or the manifest honesty of my countenance, satisfies them, for I have never had the least trouble in passing my luggage, though I have frequently seen other ladies' trunks turned topsy-turvy, and searched from one end to the other.

The journey to Madrid is of course much less fatiguing now that the railway is opened the whole way; but I could not help contrasting the first part of it, at least, unfavourably with our diligence-drive across the Pyrenees last year. The scenery is very beautiful; but, of course, just when you come to the finest spots the train rushes howling into a tunnel. We had the carriage to ourselves, and so were able to fly about from one window to another as the view was alternately to be seen from the right side or the left; but it was the pursuit of the picturesque under difficulties, and we felt rather like shuttlecocks.

I found the route by the Northern Railway altogether more interesting than my last railway journey to Madrid; but I dare say a good deal of that arose from the fact that I was prepared for the kind of landscape I was to pass through, and, you know, "Blessed are they that have no expectations." San Sebastian is a very picturesque-looking place, and so is Pasage, with its landlocked bay and steep wooded banks. It is quite the thing for the English visitors at Biarritz to go across the mountains to San Sebastian, and fancy they have been in Spain; there is no greater mistake; it is much more a French than a Spanish town, and from it you could form no idea of the rest of the country.

The scenery as you pass through the Guadarrama Mountains, is fine; but they look wonderfully barren; and, on the whole, I think I prefer them from a distance, as we used to see them from Madrid, with all the glory of their sunset colouring, than at close quarters. The railway passes quite near to the Escorial, of which you get a very good view. It is all I am likely to see of it, for neither Henry nor I care very much for sightseeing, and all who have been to the Escorial have come back declaring it to be rather a "sell"; moreover you have to start from Madrid about four o'clock in the morning to see it.

We found such a party of friends waiting for us at the station of the Northern Railway in Madrid that it felt quite homely, and I was really glad to see the old place again. As we drove through the Puerta del Sol, the same identical crowd seemed to be lounging there as when I had left it a year ago, and the clock on the government offices was still showing a different time on each of its three faces.

LETTER XI.

MADRID, *August* 31, 1865.

I WAS so glad to receive the budget of home letters, and find you were all well. We have come into the midst of very hot weather here, though it happened to be quite cool the day we arrived, fortunately for us. The windows are all closed about eight o'clock in the morning, and the venetians also, so that the rooms are almost dark. Even with these precautions, we cannot keep the thermometer lower than 84°. The other day we opened one of the windows when the sun was off it, just to see if it really kept the room cooler to have them shut, and in a few minutes the mercury went up to 90°; so we were glad to close it again.

But in the evening they are all opened wide, and remain so all night. It is very delicious then, the air is so cool and refreshing; and just now we have such splendid moonlight that we sit without lamps; and last night I was reading the 'Times' out in the balcony for a long time with the greatest ease. But even when there is no moon, in these clear southern skies the stars make it quite light. I am never tired of watching them; the blue of the heavens looks so intense, and the constellations so large and brilliant. Last night Henry and I could not go to bed, but remained talking in the balcony till nearly half-past two.

I find wonderful improvements in Madrid. The old Inglaterra was broken up while I was here last, as the house belonged to the Government, and was wanted for the French Legation; but now there is a "Grand Hôtel de Paris," at the corner of the Carera San Gerónimo, looking into the Puerta del Sol, in the place of a row of tumble-down tenements that used to stand there. At this establishment I believe the charges are very grand indeed, to suit the outside appearance; but a good hotel was greatly wanted in Madrid, for, after the death of the Inglaterra, there was not a single decent one. At one, which was considered better than the rest, an English lady who was staying there told me she always put on her galoshes and tucked up her dress to go down to dinner, because the stairs were so dirty.

The old Plaza Mayor is transformed into a garden, where statues or fountains are to be placed by-and-by. Most of the gates of the city are being pulled down, and new streets are being laid out outside the walls, though the people complain that no one will ever live in them because they are such an immense distance from the theatres! I should think they must be nearly two miles from the furthest of them, and half a mile from the nearest! Outside the Alcalá gate, and beyond the bull-ring, there is a new "Campos Elíseos," with a large square theatre in it and a piece of ornamental water, etc. etc.,—I suppose a kind of Cremorne, only that it is proper for ladies to go here. These gardens were just commenced when I was here before, and it is perfectly wonderful to see what a year has done in making the desert blossom as a rose. Already the trees look quite respectable, and in a few years they will be a great ornament to Madrid. It only shows what the soil is capable of with water.

But the greatest improvement of all is bringing the water from the Guadarrama Mountains for the use of Madrid. The streets are now watered twice a day with a hose, as it is done in Paris; it is extraordinary what a difference it makes in the air, which is no longer so dry and filled with fine dust as it used to be, making your face feel like a drum-head. When the hose is playing on the pavement below our windows in the afternoon, a steam rises up which almost seems to choke you for the moment, and the flags hiss just as the bars of a grate would do under similar circumstances, but after a few minutes the air becomes sensibly cooler, and the smell of the damp ground is delicious. Formerly there was always a heavy cloud of dust, reaching far above the heads of the people, on the "Salon del Prado" in the evening, raised by the ladies' trailing petticoats, which were, indeed, almost invisible for dirt; but now the promenade is kept well watered and is very pleasant.

The canal which conveys the water from the mountains is, I believe, a very fine piece of work. It was finished a good while ago, but, I fancy, had scarcely begun to be used when I was here before,

OLD STYLE OF WATERING THE STREETS.

for then the watering of the roads was done in a most primitive style. The water-carts were merely large barrels fixed on a cart, with a piece of thick leather tubing behind, out of which the water poured in a torrent; but, in order to scatter it a little over the road, a man walked behind each cart with a rope attached to the end of the tube, which he wagged backwards and forwards, and so spread the water after a fashion; but, as the barrels did not hold very much to begin with, and were filled at the fountains by a bucketful at a time, the watering process was neither very rapid nor very effective.

COUNTRY WOMAN ON HER DONKEY.

Only a few of the new houses have water laid on. Most people are still supplied by the water-carriers, who are paid so much a pail, or, rather, barrel. Under these circumstances water is still rather a dear commodity in Madrid.

The water-carriers are all Gallegos (natives of Galicia), and seem quite a separate class, wearing a different dress. You see them congregating in great numbers round the different fountains, generally passing the time in quarrelling while their barrels are filling, or while they are waiting for their turn. The day of San Isidro, who is their patron saint, is their great fiesta of the year; and I believe that on one occasion the saint, contrary to his usual custom, had given them a wet day, so a crowd of these Gallegos went to his church, which is the principal one in Madrid, and smashed the windows and did as much damage as they could before the civil guards dispersed them. The people have such curious ideas about their saints here,—it is undoubtedly the image itself to which they pray, and which they punish when he is not propitious.

I heard of a servant-girl the other day who had been praying for a long time to San Antonio to give her a *novio* (sweetheart), and, finding the saint deaf to all her entreaties, she took the little image she had of him, tied a string round its neck, and hung it in a well, saying, "There now; you shall stay there till you give me what I want." Some time after she did pick up a *novio* somewhere, so San Antonio was drawn up and reinstated on his altar, and even had some tallow candles burned under his nose as a treat.

We have a "tertulia" once a week, after the Spanish fashion. It is a very pleasant way of seeing one's friends, especially as it does away with the necessity of morning calls. You give a general invitation, and people come whenever they feel inclined, sometimes dropping in after the opera is over, for the Madrileño is decidedly a night bird. You are not expected to give any refreshment, except, perhaps, water, with a flavoured sugarstick to stir it with. This part of the custom, however, does not agree with English ideas of hospitality, so we infringe slightly on it; but at a Spanish house the most you ever get is a cup of chocolate, which is made as thick as mud, and is eaten by dipping Savoy biscuits into it. The cups are very small, and a glass of water is always handed with them, as the chocolate makes you very thirsty. When we have enough people for a dance we generally get one up; at other times we have music and conversation.

I have not been to any really Spanish tertulias yet, but we have some invitations. It seems it is the custom in Spain for the persons who arrive at a new place to send cards to all those whom they may wish to visit with, instead of the old residents calling on a new-comer, as with us in country places.

It is called "offering your house," and is so in fact, the proper form being to announce that "Los Señores" So-and-so have taken a house in such a street, which they place at your disposal. If you wish to know them, you call; and if not, you let it alone. Sometimes they only send a card, with the address, and this is done by every fresh family which comes into the house, so that, as some of the flats in ours have changed hands several times, we have received a good many of them. We do not, however, call in return, but merely send cards, and there the civility ends.

I find Madrid a much pleasanter place now that

I have so many more lady friends. I can go out much more than I used to do, and am not wholly dependent on riding for exercise. The C——s come very often to see me, and take me off with them for a walk in the Retiro, or a shopping expedition.

If you hire a carriage in Madrid, you are so stylish that your best friends would not recognize you. A grand barouche and pair dashes up to the door, with a Duke's coronet on the panels. The coachman and footman wear cockades, and when you appear at the door of the house, they both take off their hats, and keep them off till you are seated in the carriage. Every time you dismount the same ceremony takes place, the coachman on his box holding his hat in his hand, while the footman, also uncovered, lets down the steps, or shuts them up again, as the case may be. They never address you without raising their hat, so that you feel tremendously grand. To be sure, the carriage is rather shaky, and the linings thereof somewhat worn, while the clothes which the flunkies wear were certainly made for much larger men, and they look altogether slightly dilapidated; but then the coronet, you know, covers a multitude of sins, and the whole turn-out is not worse than that of many an old Irish family.

Spaniards have an economical way of having their servants' livery-coats made a good general size, so that they may fit any one. In their wildest moments they would never dream of having a man measured for them; for Juan, who is five feet eight, might leave to-morrow, and Pepe, who takes his place, may be only five feet two, and the same clothes must do for all comers. This is the case even in the private families.

LETTER XII.

Madrid, *September* 10.

Many of the streets still bear traces of the massacre of the 10th of April, in broken windows and smashed doors. You remember that the Civil Guards fired on a perfectly unarmed crowd, without any warning, because the students of the University had asked leave to serenade their late rector, who had been turned out of office for some speech he had made about the Queen's recent gift of part of her royal patrimony. Permission was at first granted for the serenade, and then at the last moment it was rescinded. The students had, however, assembled, and did not approve of this sudden change of mind on the part of the Government.

They did nothing worse than hiss, I believe, and hang about in knots in the streets; but the Ministers pretended to think they were mischievously inclined, and filled the Puerta del Sol with troops the two following days. On the evening of the third a great number of people had gone out to look at the troops, for no one knew why they were keeping the streets at all, and while they were quietly strolling along the pavements the order was given to fire. The regular soldiers had already, I believe, refused to do so, but the Civil Guard obeyed orders, and in a few moments numbers of the defenceless crowd were weltering in blood. Those who could fly did so, but the Guards followed them, and shot them down like rabbits. In the Cuatro Calles, a narrow paved passage connecting the Calle Alcalá with the Carera San Gerónimo, the sergeants turned all the people out of the *cafés*, and closed the doors; and before they had time to get out of the street the troops appeared at the end, and deliberately fired down it, killing almost every one in it, for there was no possibility of escape.

It was a most perfect piece of butchery, and as uncalled-for as it was brutal. Some of the incidents you hear are almost too horrible to believe. In one street, the "Espoz y Mina," a lady was standing in the balcony of her house when the firing began in the Puerta del Sol; the people rushed up the street, in their efforts to escape, and one poor man fell on her door-step, wounded by a bullet; the soldiers followed up, and one, slightly more brutal than the others, stuck his bayonet into the dying man. "For God's sake," cried the lady, "do not strike him when he is down!" For sole answer, the soldier levelled his musket at her, and shot her dead.

Three gentlemen—one of whom was an official of the Government—were shot down, just as they were entering their club, by the first volley. They were carried inside; one was dead, and another died a few hours afterwards. Henry had gone up to the club, after the streets were cleared and the firing had ceased, and there he found the wife of the dying man frantically seeking her husband, whom she knew was shot;

but the gentlemen who were in the house thought it better she should not see him, and therefore told her he was not there. Poor thing, she became quite mad, and has been so ever since. I am told she is now dying.

I cannot imagine how any people can quietly put up with such barbarities. To be sure, the ministers had to resign, and old Gonzalez Bravo, who was the one chiefly to blame, was afraid to go out without an escort for some time; but he seems to have recovered his impudence now.

A Spaniard whom I met when I was here last time, asked me how long I had been in Madrid. I replied, "Six months."—"And have you not seen a 'pronunciamiento' yet?" And on my answering in the negative, he assured me I was certain to have that pleasure before I left. I did not, however; but they take place, as a rule, I think, rather oftener than once in six months. This affair of the 10th of April, though, was no "pronunciamiento" at all, but a pure piece of butchery, unprovoked and unnecessary.

I went to my first Spanish tertulia on Tuesday

evening, and found it very pleasant; from about sixty to eighty people came in, chiefly in morning dress. It struck me as strange that, though a Spanish lady never rises to receive a gentleman, when any ladies entered the large drawing-room, where we were all seated, every one rose, while the new arrivals made the circuit of the room, shaking hands with their friends, or kissing them on both cheeks, in the French fashion, and giving an undignified little nod to those whom they did not know. The first time every one got up, I thought we were going to sing a hymn or do something extraordinary; but at last I found the ceremony had to be repeated so often that I began to wish all the guests would arrive together. However, it was discontinued as soon as the dancing began, which was as soon as a sufficient number had assembled to form a *rigodon*, a kind of quadrille, with all the figures curtailed.

There was a long pause between each dance; but it was not spent by the ladies in sitting in rows round the walls, and by the gentlemen blocking up the doorways and passages, as it would have been in England; the whole company broke up into little knots and circles of ladies and gentlemen. The numerous chairs which were pushed into the corners or into the ante-room while the dance was going on, were fetched out, and the gentlemen generally seated themselves in front of the ladies, and kept up a lively conversation until the music struck up again for the next waltz.

I was much amused by listening to the conversation around me. There were but very few old ladies playing propriety, and these sat on the same spot all evening, and talked about their houses—how much rent they paid, how many windows and chimneys they had,—and asked each other whether they burned coal or wood. They reminded me of the "two crumbly old women" in Longfellow's 'Kavanagh,' who talked about "moths and cheap furniture, and the best cure for rheumatism."

As for the talk of the young people, it was so small as to be almost invisible, though it was by no means inaudible; it was absolutely about nothing; and yet it never ceased, and they all appeared perfectly satisfied with each other.

I am very glad to have an opportunity of going into a little society among the Spaniards, and I like them very much—that is to say, the women; for the men I do not like at all. From the time they emerge from petticoats into cloth clothes, they have more than the ordinary impudence of a grown-up man, and as "pollos" they are insufferable,—it is only the old men who are at all nice, and not very many of them. But the ladies have exceedingly pleasant, frank manners, like those of Irishwomen, and they, one and all, seem wonderfully free from affectation. There were a great many pretty girls in the room the other evening, but I did not see one who was conceited. Fernan Caballero, the best Spanish novelist of the present day, has a long dissertation in one of her books (I think 'Clemencia') on the simplicity of the Spanish women, who, she says, never practise dissimulation, or attempt to appear other than they are; and she goes on to hope that this frankness and absence of pretension will not be driven out by French manners, as the "saya" and "mantilla" have already given way before the invasion of French bonnets and mantles "without our women remembering that each artificial grace deprives them of a real one, each affectation of a charm, and that from graceful and fresh natural flowers they will convert themselves into stiff and formal artificial ones."

I do not think this eulogium is overdrawn; the Spanish women are, as she says, free from any attempt to appear anything but what they are, and it is a great charm in them; but it is like the innocence of Eve,—it never seems to occur to them that they could be improved; they are so perfectly satisfied with themselves as they are that there is nothing to wish for—nothing to affect.

About twelve o'clock tea was to be had in one of the rooms; but that was the only refreshment provided, though dancing was still going on when we left at one o'clock. The rooms were in a stifling state of heat, for no windows were open, and there was a thick curtain always kept drawn over the door; but no one but ourselves seemed to find it too warm, or to think the air bad, though it was so thick that you could scarcely see across the room.

September 20, 1865.

We heard a story the other day illustrative of Spanish railway management. A friend of ours was coming up to Madrid by the Northern Railway; at one of the wayside stations, after waiting the usual half-hour while all the officials had their smoke, the signal was given for starting, and the engine had given its preliminary shriek, when two of the porters on the platform began to fight. Such a sight as this was not to be lost, and the train was kept back until it was over; "and," said our friend, "I should not have minded if it had been a good stand-up fight, but, after all, they only slapped each other's faces like a couple of school-girls, and we lost a quarter of an hour watching them."

I have learned a great deal more about Spanish customs lately, since I understood the language better and had so many more friends here. I wish very much to see the ceremony of a nun taking the veil, and several people have promised to let me know when there is an opportunity of seeing one; but it seems to be such a common occurrence that they make no fuss about it. Marriages are conducted very differently from ours. If the ceremony is performed in church, the bride and all the ladies are dressed in black, for which reason fashionable people are now introducing the custom of being married in the house, where they can display a more lively costume. The marriage takes place in the evening, and I believe the newly married couple do not leave the bride's house, except when the husband's house is in the same town; but they do not go off on a wedding-tour in any circumstances. A second ceremony of some sort takes place in the church, but it need not follow immediately on the other; and, indeed, it is considered enough if it is performed any time before the birth of the first child.

It is at this religious rite that the ring is given, if given at all; but it is no part of the ceremony, and you see quite as many Spanish wives without a wedding-ring as with,— nor when worn is it by any means generally a plain gold one, as with us, but oftener a fancy ring of some sort. The bride provides all the house linen for the new establishment, and is expected to give her husband, as a wedding-gift, at least six new shirts, which are generally extremely fine and elaborately embroidered. Among the poorer classes the wife provides the bed and bedding. The husband assists in furnishing the bride's trousseau, giving her, generally, all her most handsome dresses, including the wedding-dress itself when the ceremony is to be performed in the house, and she can appear in something sufficiently gorgeous.

Fernan Caballero devotes some pages in one of her novels to show how very preferable is the Spanish mode of conducting marriages, and how very abominable is the practice of English brides and bridegrooms in starting off on a journey among strangers on the day of their wedding: exposing themselves, as she says, "to the jeers of postilions and stable-boys," instead of remaining among friends. But, alas for Spain! which this extremely conservative writer would fain warn against the malpractices of other countries, it is already becoming "the thing" for fashionable people to spend their honeymoon or, as the Spaniards have it, "eat their wedding-cake," in a tour of some sort.

Although marriages are frequently made up entirely by parents and guardians, and, in some cases, without the two people most interested in the arrangement having even seen each other, custom, or law, gives a woman much more power in Spain in these matters than in England. If she does not approve of the choice made for her, and her parents wish to coerce her, she has only to apply for protection to a magistrate, who will even take her out of her father's house, if she wishes it, until she is of age and her own mistress. But, more than that, if a girl wishes to marry a man whom her parents disapprove, however good may be their reasons for refusing their consent, she has only to place herself under the protection of the magistrate to set them at defiance,—nor have they, I believe, any power to deprive her of the portion, which by Spanish law falls to her share, of the family property. Nor are the Spanish ladies slow to avail themselves of this liberty. I have heard of several marriages which have been made in this way, and of one case where the first intimation the father received of his daughter's engagement was a notice from a neighbouring magistrate that she was about to be married. In another case, a daughter left her mother's house, because she would not consent to her marriage with a man without income and considerably beneath her in rank, and was married from that of the magistrate; the mother at the last, however, could not resist sending her a wedding-dress and going to see the ceremony.

Many of these matches are made up from chance meetings in the street or theatre, and the wooing is carried on through the "reja," or the balcony, after the family are all in bed; or by means of a clandestine correspondence, under cover to the maid. This is the natural result of the extreme strictness which is outwardly observed in their conduct, no unmarried lady being allowed to entertain a gentleman alone for a moment; nor are engaged couples, under any circumstances, left alone together. A Spanish lady, who was staying in England for some time, quarrelled and separated from an English girl, who had been one of her dearest friends, because, when at some flower-show or *fête*, she and one of the gentlemen of the party became accidentally separated from the rest, and walked home together, arriving some five minutes later than the others; and on telling Henry the story, she expressed her very great astonishment at finding that the parents of the girl could see no harm in what she had done, and actually upheld her.

When a woman marries, she does not lose her maiden name, but adds that of her husband, with "de" prefixed. If her husband dies, she resumes her own name, and is called "Viuda de Fulano," widow of So-and-so. Children bear the name of both parents, the father's first; thus a woman, whose maiden name was Clemencia Lopez, becomes, on marriage, Clemencia Lopez de Martiñez; and her children are called Martiñez y Lopez; and if she becomes a widow, she is Clemencia Lopez, Viuda de Martiñez. Every one is called by their Christian name, even by young children. Almost the first thing you are asked is your name, and you then become Maria or

Isabel, or whatever it may chance to be, to every one. Frequently they are rendered into a diminutive, and Francisca becomes Paca or Paquita, and Josefa, Pepa or Pepita. Gentlemen are generally addressed by their surname alone, as Lopez or Martinez, without any Señor or Don prefixed, unless they are known very intimately, and then the Christian name is used. Don is never placed before the surname alone; it is Don Carlos or Don Juan, but Señor Lopez, or Señor Don Juan Lopez in a formal address.

The men are very fond of embracing each other, and doing what Emerson calls "clawing." I was much amused at one of the theatres, where a piece was being played in which several Englishmen were introduced, to see the way our countrymen were represented. The distinctive mark was always a long pair of Cardigan whiskers, of a pale drab colour; and these ideal Englishmen were constantly falling on each other's neck and kissing, or walking about the stage with their arms round each other like a pair of school-girls. This, and saying "By Jove" at every other sentence, is the Spanish idea of an Englishman, though why we should be supposed to have a monopoly of swearing, I do not know; for with us, at any rate, ladies do not indulge in this propensity, while in Spain every second exclamation begins with "Por Dios," and it is as much used by ladies as by gentlemen. Going down the street one day I heard a lady say to another who was with her, "*Jésus*, we have passed the shop we wanted!"—"*Ay, por Dios*, so we have," answered her companion.

They show a singular want of reverence for sacred names or characters, constantly making joking reference to Christ, and in one of their most popular songs, the contrabandista, who is supposed to sing it, says he has a "stunning pair of whiskers, such as have never been seen since Jesus Christ's."

As a Christian name Jesus is very common, and so are Trinidad and Concepcion, which last is abbreviated into Concha.

LETTER XIII.

MADRID, *November* 21, 1865.

WE have written to you so constantly during the time of the cholera that I hope you have never been anxious about us; now I think we may almost consider it gone, and all danger over. It has, however, been an awful visitation while it lasted, and has left Madrid looking like a city of the dead. I believe there had been some cases of cholera daily from the beginning of July, but though rumours of it got about, they were diligently contradicted, by orders of the Government. The hot weather lasted unusually long, and we were all expecting an outbreak from day to day; but it was not until the seventh of October, when heavy rain commenced, that it suddenly broke out and raged furiously. There had been a few cases reported in the papers during the week; but on Sunday the eighth, when it poured from morning till night, there were one thousand and eleven deaths in the twenty-four hours; a tolerable proportion in a population of less than 400,000, was it not?

The following morning there was a regular panic in the city, and such a rush to the provinces that a detachment of soldiers had to be posted at the Northern Railway station to preserve order. In the next few days 80,000 persons had left Madrid. One man is said to have presented himself at the booking-office and demanded a ticket. "Where for?" asked the clerk. "Anywhere, anywhere," replied the other; "so that I get away from here." Of course many were seized with cholera at the miserable little villages to which they had fled for fancied security, and died there. Those who were obliged to remain were, many of them, in abject terror; they shut themselves up in their houses, and gave up eating any sort of vegetable or fruit, living entirely on meat; the consequence of which was that they were generally attacked by some other disease, and frequently died. Some people we knew filled their stockings and shoes with sulphur, kept a quill full of camphor always in their mouths, and when obliged to go out, carried a bottle of spirits of camphor with them, the contents of which they sprinkled over every place they went into. They hung up a picture of San Roqué in their room, and kept lights continually burning before it, and twice a day performed their devotions to this saint of plagues.

Another man, hearing that a good perspiration was the thing to be desired in case of cholera, and fancying that prevention was better than cure, sat before a huge fire for a week, wrapped in all the topcoats and blankets he could find, keeping his windows and doors closely shut; "and notwithstanding all that, I find myself very weak," he remarked to a friend of ours.

What can you expect from such people? Is it not better they should die, and make room for sensible people? The strange thing is, however, that these cowards are not the ones who die. Remembering the old story about cholera killing one thousand, and fear killing ten thousand, we naturally expected to hear of their being down next; but I noticed that this prolonged terror of the disease did not seem to bring it on. It generally attacked those who had had a sudden shock, either from losing a friend, or seeing some one seized in the streets,—what servants call " getting a turn,"—but who had not previously thought much about the cholera.

The Prado was utterly deserted,—we used not to see a soul when we were riding,—and the streets were almost equally so. In the Puerta del Sol, where you can generally scarcely push your way through the crowds on the pavement, there were rarely a dozen people to be seen, and the *cafés* were left empty at night. During the first few days of the outbreak fires were kept burning in the middle of the streets, but it was supposed that they increased the terror of the people, and they were discontinued. The priests were forbidden to ring a bell when taking the sacrament to the dying, and bodies were removed at night, so as to keep the ravages the epidemic was making as quiet as possible.

Some persons who remained behaved most nobly, forming themselves in societies for visiting and tending the sick. I heard of one priest who went into a wretched cellar, and found a poor child in all the agonies of cholera, while his father and mother lay dead beside him; after trying in vain for some time to bring warmth into the poor little body, he got into the miserable bed, and took the child into his arms, and so saved his life. A man who had been most active in visiting one of the worst quarters of Madrid, told a friend of ours that the mortality among children was awful; that when they were attacked, no one seemed to think of trying to save them; and that their bodies used to be carried out to the dead-carts in basketfuls at a time at night. I think the doctors must have killed quite as many as the cholera did; for in some cases they bled their patients, and, in most cases, when the active symptoms were curbed, kept them without food until they died of what they called typhus. We had fully determined that if either of us were taken ill we would have no doctor, but would trust entirely to chlorodyne. Henry treated a great many people with it, and in every case was successful; even in the case of a woman who had been for six hours down with a most malignant attack, and had had no remedies applied. In stopping cholera in its first stages, we found it invaluable.

We were so surrounded by the epidemic at one time, and so many people we knew were seized, that if we did not see any of our friends for a couple of days, we became quite anxious about them, and sent to inquire. Many deaths were so sudden, and the burials so private, that people who lost friends never heard of it until long after. Now that the worst is over, we really hear more of it than we did at the time; but the people are beginning to come out again, and the place does not look so dreadful as it has been doing. The shopkeepers say they are selling nothing but mourning and "habits;" these habits are the dress of some religious orders, which ladies make a vow to wear for a certain length of time, if the Virgin will only hear their prayers. So many people made these vows in their terror that there is little else to be seen now in the way of ladies' dress; but many of them remind you of the old couplet,—

"When the devil fell sick, the devil a saint would be;
When the devil got well, the devil a saint was he;"

for they are so fashionably made that you would never discover they were habits at all; and the leather strap, which is always part of the costume, is frequently kept quite out of sight beneath the folds of the dress,—I believe in some cases the priest has refused to give the necessary blessing when some superfashionable robe has been presented for his sanction.

For ourselves, we never made the least change in our way of living, took our usual quantity of vegetables and fruit, and went out every day, only avoiding passing unnecessarily through the places where the epidemic was worst; it has, however, been a very terrible time, and one we are not likely to forget soon.

There was to have been a grand bull-fight on Tuesday last for the benefit of the sufferers from cholera, and our English friends, who are now here, had taken a box. They persuaded me to go to see the Plaza fill with people, and the entrance of the procession of the toreros, horses, mules, etc. etc., into the arena, and Henry had promised to bring me out before the fight began. However, the whole affair was put off in consequence of the ground being so slippery from the rain as to make it dangerous for the men; so we went to the picture gallery instead, and I am quite sure I enjoyed it much more, for I had a horror that if I were once in the Plaza I might be let in for some of the fight, and I have no fancy for any such butchery.

We have made acquaintance lately with the Casa de Campo, which, as I think I told you, is a royal property lying on the opposite side of the river from Madrid. There is a miserable tumble-down old house in it, which goes by the name of a palace, to which strangers are admitted by cards one day in the week; but there is nothing to see, and the only interest it has is an historical one, for it was there Charles I., when Prince of Wales, went to see his intended bride, and, climbing over the garden wall, dropped down at her feet, regardless of the horrified propriety of her attendants. For right to ride in the park you require an order from the King himself; but though one of our friends had been kind enough to procure one for us, we had never thought it worth while making use of it until a short time ago, when, on exploring the place a little, we were surprised to find it of very great extent, and very beautiful, for Madrid. It is a capital place for riding in, as in addition to plenty of good, sound turf, the roads, which cross the park in every direction, are as soft for the horses' feet as Rotten Row.

We had all arranged to have a long ride there on Sunday, but when the day arrived, there was a thick white fog over everything, which reminded us of England, certainly, but was not otherwise agreeable. Some of our party turned soft and thought it foolish to go out at all, but four of us were courageous enough to start, and we were amply rewarded. One part of the park lies on a long, high ridge, and the ground slopes gradually down from it to the river. Just as we reached this high point the sun broke out, and as the mist cleared away little by little, resting here and there in the hollows, and finally disappearing entirely, we had a splendid view across the sloping park, with its groves of ilex and pine, to where the river was just visible, winding through the golden trees. Beyond it the ground rose again, and far away to our right was Madrid, on the edge of the steep cliff at the foot of which winds the Manzanares. It looked like an Eastern city, with the domes of its innumerable churches cut clearly out against a deep blue sky, and not a thread of smoke to be seen rising from it. The windows were glittering in the sunlight like diamonds, and, as it was the day of the Te Deum for the departure of the cholera, the sound of church bells came, softened by the distance, across the wide valley to where we stood resting beneath some splendid pine-trees. Opposite to us, beyond the river, was the Florida—a well-planted park, with grass as green as I ever saw it in Ireland in springtime,—forming the most charming foreground to the Guadarramas, which stretched away as far as you could see, losing themselves in a purple haze at last. They are now just crested with snow, and it was beautiful to watch their changing tints as the sun sank behind the high ground on the other side of Madrid and the rosy light faded into grey,— and the highest peaks were still bathed in golden sunshine, while the lower portions were turning from grey to deep purple.

I spoke just now of golden trees:—it is no figure of speech, for the leaves are still on the beeches and are of the most glorious amber-colour just now. I never saw autumn tints so strangely bright; they give all the appearance of sunlight even in the shady places, and when the sun is on them, they seem to be of burnished gold, and look wonderfully beautiful, mixed with the dark-leaved ilex and sombre olive.

If you are at all able to picture the scene to yourself from my meagre description, you will easily imagine that we found it difficult to tear ourselves away, and longed for fresh horses to go on riding for a couple of hours longer.

When you remember that Madrid was originally chosen as a royal residence on account of the forests which surrounded it, and that the stupid inhabitants have cut down every tree they could lay their hands on for firewood, you feel inclined to pound in a mortar the people who have turned what must have been one of the richest and most beautiful parts of Spain, or, indeed, of Europe, into an arid, blazing desert, which looks for all the world like the back of a mangy dromedary.

I suppose you have seen the letters in the 'Times,' from "Our Special Correspondent;" they are very good, indeed, and not at all overdrawn. Since his letter about the tiresome custom-house regulations here, a new royal order has come out that passengers' luggage is not to be molested unless there is an unusual supply of new clothes in it. Formerly everything that had not been worn was liable to pay duty, and in some cases it used to be enforced. Personally I have nothing to complain of, for I got off free of any annoyance; but one lady I know was charged £9 duty on her dresses alone.

The Spaniards are very angry, however, at some of the things that have been said about their Queen; for though they speak of her themselves constantly in the most disrespectful way, they do not like a foreigner to say a word that is not in praise of anything and everything Spanish. The fiction of her respectability is kept up in the funniest way in the public papers, while in private the greatest licence is used in speaking of her.

LETTER XIV.

Madrid, *January* 5, 1866.

I hope you were not alarmed by the account in the 'Times' of Prim's insurrection. Henry wrote a few lines to tell you there was nothing to fear for us, as we are quite out of the way of any disturbance there might be.

Though every one had been talking of a revolution for the last six months, and the 'Times' correspondent had been representing it as imminent, no one believed it to be any nearer than it had been for months past, and we were really quite taken by surprise. Henry and I had been out after breakfast on the 1st of January, and were in a shop in the Calle Alcalá, when we saw O'Donnell and his staff go past in full dress. We are, however, so accustomed to reviews and all kinds of military displays here that we thought nothing of it, and Henry left me at the house of a friend, and went on to his office. In a few minutes a gentleman came to say Henry had sent him to take me home, as a revolution had broken out, and the streets would not be safe. He told me Prim had left Madrid early in the morning with two cavalry regiments, which were to be joined by two more from Alcalá; that troops had been dispatched in pursuit; and that all the public offices were closed. Every one was hurrying home with a lively recollection of the April massacres, and I was very glad to see Henry come in a few minutes after I reached the house. A detachment of cavalry was then riding round the city, proclaiming martial law in all the Plazas, and in a short time troops began marching down the Prado on their way to follow the insurgents. All that day and night there was great excitement, for Prim was supposed to be marching on Madrid, and we were listening for firing. However, none was heard, and in the morning it appeared that the two regiments in Alcalá had failed to rise, as they had agreed; and Prim, after vainly waiting for them as long as he dared, and knowing it was useless to attempt Madrid with so few troops, had turned off to Aranjuez. We have not been able to gain any real information as to his movements, for, of course, the government reports are not to be believed; but it is thought that he is lingering somewhere within reach of Madrid, in hopes of a general rising in the city. Other reports say that he is moving towards Zaragoza and Barcelona, which he hopes will declare in his favour. Here, in Madrid, no troops are about the streets; they are all kept in barracks, and the town is in the hands of the Civil Guard, the fact being that the Government does not know what regiments may be trusted. The Artillery are supposed to be loyal, but I think they have not much confidence even in them. The Guards at the Palace, and the Government offices in the Puerta de Sol, are formed of a few men out of several different corps, mixed with Civil Guards. The casino, or club, is closed, and the *cafés* are ordered to be emptied at nine o'clock in the evening;

but this seems to be an unnecessary regulation, as scarcely any one goes near them; now, and at night, the streets are entirely deserted; indeed, during the daytime, very few people go out, and only those who have business go into the town. Ladies are, of course, all close prisoners, for there are constant reports that the soldiers have risen in one or other of the barracks, or that the people are up in such a quarter, and are raising barricades. When one of these reports gets about, every one begins to hurry home; cabs and carriages go off at full speed for fear of being used for the barricades, and in a few minutes there is a regular flight; every one running, without knowing from what. This is succeeded by a dead calm: the shopkeepers have hurriedly put up their shutters, and closed their doors; every one has disappeared, and left the empty streets to the dominion of the Civil Guard, who are everywhere patrolling them. It is thought that these "runs," as they are called, are got up by the insurrectionary party, in the hope of inducing the Guards to fire on them, and so initiate the revolution; but if so, O'Donnell is too wise to allow them to do so. The troops do not fire, but evidently have orders to disperse the people as quietly as possible.

Yesterday a different alarm was raised in four separate parts of Madrid, and the people, in their flight from the imaginary danger, rushed towards the Puerta del Sol, where the four streams met, and produced a scene of the utmost confusion,— every one struggling to get home by the nearest way before the troops should fire on them. We heard the scene was most extraordinary; the sea of heads surging hither and thither, and emptying itself as best it could by the numerous streets which lead from the grand square. One friend of ours who was passing at the time was taken completely off his feet and carried for some distance, until he managed to get into a doorway and let the crowd pass. Meanwhile, the soldiers were merely driving the people off the pavement with their bayonets and compelling them to move on. Narvaez or Gonzalez Bravo would certainly have fired on them, but O'Donnell does not seem to wish to shed unnecessary blood, and, besides, will not needlessly be the first to come to blows. We cannot, of course, ride; nor, indeed, do we send the horses out to exercise: for if Prim be in the neighbourhood, and there is any rising in the town,—an event which may take place at any moment,—they might be seized by the insurgents. If any one but O'Donnell were at the head of affairs, I could heartily wish Prim success, but as he seems to be the only man able to govern at all, I see no advantage to be had by upsetting him.

For many months past the Progresista papers have been talking very big of the revolution that was coming: only let some one take the initiative and the world should see what wonders they would work,—what fine fellows they were. Let some one be ready to lead them and almost all Spain would rise and follow; and now Prim has gone out with his life in his hand, and not one of these trumpeting gentlemen seems inclined to come out of his shell; they have suddenly grown dumb and wonderfully quiet. The people, indeed, appear perfectly unconcerned; to shrug their shoulders is the utmost sign of interest they give. They do not care a straw which side wins so long as they have plenty of paper cigars, and they can take the sun in peace and quietness.

January 19, 1866.

We are still in the same pleasant state of uncertainty here: still under martial law, and I, at least, am unable to get out any distance from home, for it is not safe for ladies to be in the street now on account of the "runs" which are always taking place. Every day since Prim went out we have been told in the strictest confidence that the revolution was to begin that night. The porter of the house has been in a chronic state of terror, and is always closing the outer gates and rushing up, with a white face, to tell us there is firing going on in some of the streets. For the first ten days we were always going into the balcony to listen for this same firing, and two nights, when it had seemed unusually certain the great event was to come off, we sat up till between two and three o'clock in the morning; but after so many false cries of "wolf" we have become quite savage, and have posted up a notice over the mirror in the drawing-room, "Il est défendu de parler de la révolution." One night an alarm was given, and in a few minutes all the theatres and the opera-house were emptied, the people flying home as best they might,—of course it was nothing; and you have no notion how extremely absurd it is to see one of these runs. First come cabs and carriages rattling past at full gallop, then a troop of men tearing along with their long cloaks flying behind them, making them look like terrified bats; after every one is safely housed, and not a living soul is to be seen in the streets but the inevitable Civil Guards, they begin to ask each other what they were running for,—" Because you ran," is the only answer; but who first begins the scamper no one seems to know.

It is no wonder, though, that people should be frightened, knowing what has happened before; and the last proclamation which has come out is, that any four people found standing together in the street may be fired on by the troops; so, when they find a crowd of persons running towards them, they naturally take to their heels for fear of the consequences.

Yesterday the first blood was shed in the persons of two sergeants, who were shot at eight o'clock in the morning, O'Donnell himself sitting by in his carriage,—fancy what a treat for him before breakfast! It seemed so horrible when we heard of it, for it was such a lovely morning, with a clear, peaceful sky, and a balmy, summer-like air, and one could not help fancying the scene in all its horrible contrast to the day;—and then this is not an insurrection as we understand the word, but only the Spanish way of changing the Ministry. If Prim succeeds and the Progresistas come into power, these poor fellows are not traitors but martyrs, and their execution is a murder; and, besides, they have only done what O'Donnell himself taught them to do in 1856, and so raised himself to his present position,—I wished heartily that the firing-party had turned round and shot the old wolf himself as he sat in his carriage. The place chosen, too, for the execution is close to the Fuente Castellano, where all the fashionables were driving and showing off their finery in the afternoon of the same day; for the brave inhabitants of this "heroic" city, as they call it, are beginning to come out again as usual, though at night the streets are still deserted and the taverns and *cafés* obliged to be closed by twelve o'clock.

Prim seems to have no idea of giving up yet, and there are fresh accounts every day of risings in the provinces, Zaragoza and Lérida on Wednesday, and Valencia yesterday; but we can gain no real information, for the papers are not allowed to publish anything that has not been first submitted to a Government censor. It is said the insurgents are retreating towards Portugal, but few people believe it. We had laid in a stock of provisions at the beginning of the disturbances, as, if there had been a rising here, we could not have got any; but all danger of that kind is over now.

Gonzalez Bravo has always a couple of Civil Guards to protect him, wherever he goes, as he is in terror of his life, if the people rise. During the first ten days he was quite invisible, and every one said his house would be the first attacked. They say the Civil Guards are very much discontented, because they are detested by the people on account of the massacre of San Daniel (April 10, 1865), and now they are just as unpopular with the soldiers, whom they are set to watch, so that in case of a general insurrection they would be the first to be massacred. They, however, are alone to be depended on; the army is so completely disorganized that they dare not let the troops that are supposed to be pursuing Prim come within sight of the insurgents, for fear they should go over to them in a body.

February 8, 1866.

All our grand Revolution has collapsed—ended in the merest smoke; and though we are still in a state of siege, no one would find it out, for everything goes on just as usual, except that the casino is still closed, to the great disgust of the gentlemen. O'Donnell only appears to keep on the martial law to be able to shoot offenders and keep the Liberal papers in check. Angry as I was with him for shooting the two sergeants for following the example he had himself set them, I do not think that he has shed more blood than he could well help (considering he is a Spaniard) in crushing this rebellion; Narvaez or Bravo would have fired on the people a dozen times in the same circumstances. As it is, only three have been shot; and I suppose, however O'Donnell gained his power, now that he is at the head, he must preserve discipline and order if he can. The third man who was shot was the captain who was to have taken out the two regiments of cavalry from Alcalá to join Prim. He had the men all equipped and ready to start, but at the last moment wavered and sent them all to bed again, determining to wait until he should hear that Prim had actually left Madrid. Meanwhile O'Donnell got some inkling of the affair, and appeared himself at Alcalá, and took off both regiments to Madrid, where they were disarmed and kept prisoners in one of the barracks. The captain was one of those officers sent in pursuit of Prim, and it was during his absence that papers were found in the possession of the sergeants which implicated him. On his return he was arrested, and was condemned to death. Great efforts were made to obtain a pardon for him; several of the foreign ministers in Madrid petitioned for him, and even the Queen herself asked O'Donnell to spare him; but he replied that if her Majesty chose to exercise her prerogative she could pardon him herself, but that in that case he must resign. The Queen, though she has no liking for O'Donnell, could not spare him in such a crisis, and the poor captain was left to die; even a last appeal, made by his wife to the council of ministers, was useless. I do not see how his life could have been spared, after shooting the sergeants; for, if they were guilty, the man who instigated and was to have led them was still more so; and I was the less sorry for him that it was by his vacillation that the whole enterprise miscarried; for there is no doubt that, had Prim had the other two regiments, the rest of the army would have gone over to him. It was given out when the two sergeants were shot, that they had intended to let loose two thousand prisoners of the worst class in Alcalá, but it was a fabrication to excuse the execution. Nevertheless, the people have put a little black cross and a heap of stones on the spot where each was shot, which is the usual way of marking where a murder has taken place. It was very horrible altogether, and we are very thankful that there are no more to be killed.

One can take no sort of interest in these "pronunciamientos," for one can see no good to be gained by them. Certainly Spain is badly enough governed now, but it would be no better if the Progresista party held the reins. Each minister as he comes into power thinks only of filling his own pockets; such a thing as public spirit, let alone patriotism, does not exist; and after all O'Donnell seems to be the only man who can manage the people; he knows exactly when to threaten and when to cajole them; he is accustomed to their blustering courage, and knows it will melt away at the first sign of danger to their own precious skins. He is extremely popular with the army, though no personal favourite of the Queen, as indeed he is not likely to be, when his first effort on coming into power is to get rid of the crowd of priests and favourites who govern her. I cannot help admiring the man, to a certain extent, for his determination and firmness: he is no more public-spirited than any other Spaniard,—I believe Number One is with him also the first, if not the only, consideration—but he is far-seeing, and knows which way the tide is running, and will take advantage of it. He is never needlessly brutal or bloodthirsty, like Narvaez, though nothing stops him which comes between him and the fulfilment of his purposes. On the whole, he is probably the most enlightened ruler Spain has at present, for every one agrees in saying that though Espartero is the one honest man in the country, he has no administrative talent and is never fit to hold the helm; and the Progresistas seem to want everything that could bind them together and give them solidity as a party. One cannot help being sorry for Prim, for if ever a man was tempted to rebellion by the encouragements of his party he was; and, once out, they abandoned him in the most cowardly manner, and left him to make the best of his escape to Portugal. Of course he has been deprived of all his honours, and sentenced to death, whenever he may be caught; but people here shrug their shoulders and say, "Oh, he will be back here in a couple of years, as great a man as ever." His wife has only just left Madrid, to join him in Paris. She was driving about on the Prado every day during the time her husband was being chased by the royal troops, and went to take leave of the Queen before leaving. The Queen would not sign the decree depriving Prim of his honours, until he was actually out of the country, for fear she might have to restore them all to him in a day or two, and add several new ones to them.

We see O'Donnell very often; he is a tall, well-made man, head and shoulders over almost every one in Madrid, and shows his Irish extraction very plainly, being utterly unlike a Spaniard in every way, as far as appearance goes. He has those excessively blue eyes, whose colour is visible even at a distance, a cruelly determined mouth, and a great square jaw, like a prize-fighter. He is a man, one could not pass without noticing, for I never saw a face which betokened such an iron will; and yet there is an incongruity about it, for his brow is open and his eyes have a good-humoured twinkle about them that goes oddly with the heavy jaw, and would seem to suit some amiable old Paterfamilias better than him.

The chase after Prim was the veriest farce, for the great end to be attained was to prevent the pursuers coming up with the pursued. On one occasion, when Echagüe and his troops arrived at the railway station of one of the villages, Prim, with his staff around him, was seen quietly standing in the street, and while the royalist soldiers were getting out of the train, he went composedly on to join his men, who were a little in advance; considering that the captain who was to have brought out the Alcalá regiments was commanding part of the troop in pursuit, it was no unnecessary precaution to keep them separate. The army is said to be in a fearfully demoralized state; there is scarcely a regiment which can be trusted, and they are obliged to divide them and set one corps to watch another. The artillery are supposed to be faithful, but they alone.

Gonzalez Bravo has been in a tremendous fright during these disturbances, never stirring except under the protection of two Civil Guards, and he has had sentinels posted at the door of his private house. If there had been a rising, he would have been one of the first victims to the popular vengeance, if he could have been found; but he used great precautions to ensure concealment, in case of necessity. He is a most disagreeable-looking man, with all the sneaking, bloodthirsty look of a baffled wolf. Narvaez, who is a great favourite with the Queen, is not much better, and is detested by the people. I shall be heartily glad if both fall into the hands of the populace in some of these hundred and fifty "pronunciamientos," and receive the due reward of their deeds. Bravo, some years ago, had occasion to shoot a priest who had been paying an affectionate attention to the spiritual welfare of his wife, and immediately after the crime he gave himself up to the police; but the powers that be, considering the circumstances of the murder and the rank and sanctity of the victim, thought it was better quietly to remove the body and say nothing about the affair.

The Duchess of Frias (*née* Balfe, late Crampton) is creating quite a sensation here by the style which she keeps up. She has an English carriage, with all the London appointments, wigged coachman, powdered and silk-stockinged footmen, etc. Such a thing has never been seen in Madrid before, and accordingly attracts much attention; she and her husband are both very handsome. It is said that she will be received at Court whenever Sir John Crampton leaves Madrid. At present she is not received, and the Duke has returned all his decorations and honours to the Queen in consequence. There is some law-suit pending between the Duke and an elder sister of his, who is trying to prove him illegitimate. If he lose the cause, he will of course have to give up all the property. Mamma Balfe is staying with her daughter, in readiness for an expected happy event.

February 10, 1865.

I am sitting writing in the balcony, where I have made a shady corner for myself with the sun-shutters, for it is such a delicious day that I really could not stay inside the room, even though all the windows were open. There has never been known such a beautiful winter here; in fact, we have had no winter; the only cold weather we had was in October, and now it is like those hot days we sometimes have in May in England, only that the sky is cloudless, and is of a blue which is unknown to our dear little misty island. We ride now at about four o'clock, and generally go to the Casa de Campo, which, as the trees are mostly evergreen-oaks, looks quite summer-like. Sometimes, if we have not time for so long a ride, we go up to some high ground, on our side of Madrid, to see the sunset, galloping up the hills to catch the last glimpse of him after he has set to the valleys. I have become quite attached to the very barrenness of the scenery here. The full view of the horizon, with the exception of the part where the Guadarramas—still tipped with snow—form a broken line, gives one all the feeling of being at sea. From our hill we look upon Madrid, lying within the line of the horizon, perfectly still and smokeless, reminding one of Elmore's or Roberts' pictures of an Eastern city; and to the east lies the valley of the Henares, stretching up past Alcalá and Guadalajara. It is the strangest valley I ever saw, having all the appearance of a huge river-bed, winding between high hills, which are broken into every imaginable shape; but all have flat tops, so that the valley seems to have sunk bodily down, leaving the old high-level distinctly traceable. As the sun gets low all this valley is in deep shadow, while the flat tops of the hills on each side are in full sunshine,—you cannot imagine how curious the effect is.

As soon as we have watched the sun disappear, we turn our horses' heads and go back to Madrid as fast as we can, as there is scarcely any twilight, and it is not pleasant to be outside the gates after dark. Caballero, in one of her books, gives a couple of pages to expatiating on the beauty of these barren Spanish landscapes, which, she declares, have a more lasting charm than any other. I laughed at the idea at first, but I acknowledge now that there is a charm in them, though it would be difficult to describe what it is, unless it is the wide horizon and the cloudless sky. I do not, however, admire a cloudless sky very much; it is much more beautiful when there are clouds to catch the varying tints of the sunset; and, except for the mountains, which are always glorious in the dying light, there is not much to be seen here.

I have read several of Caballero's books, and find them very interesting. She is half German, and has been, I believe, governess to the family of the Duchess of Montpensier; her pictures of Spanish life are excellent, the company assembled at the tertulias inimitable, with their utterly frivolous conversation, half scandalous, half inane. One thing that strikes you in Spanish society is the way that the youngest girls—mere children, even—take part in the discussion of any current scandal, going into all the particulars before the company, like any slanderous old dowager. This peculiarity is shown up and blamed in 'Clemencia,' the most interesting, and, I think, the best of Caballero's works. Indeed, this writer, though a firm believer in and lover of her country, is by no means blind to the faults of its people, many of which, however, she ascribes to French influence.

She paints the national characteristics with a loving hand, and her pictures of village life are very interesting, although they are so simple. In 'Clemencia' an English baronet is introduced, who is really no caricature, but is a very good Englishman from a foreign point of view. In the last chapter, she tells her readers that this Sir George Percy had " several statues erected to him, of various sizes, just as was done to Lord Wellington." This reward of merit appears to have been granted to him in Parliament, for his services on behalf of his country,—mainly for a rabid speech against Catholicism. With the exception, however, of this slip, he is capitally drawn, and it is amusing to see how our national traits strike foreigners.

But by far the best character in the book is a Government clerk, who at some unmentionable age is earning seventy pounds a year; those who have never been in Spain would not appreciate the truth of this portrait, but it is exact. I wish you could read it; but there is no English translation. Of these Government *employés*, a friend of ours once said to a Spaniard, " But what do they do, or have they anything to do ?"

" Oh, yes," replied his informant, " some of them have to fetch their salaries; but most of them have them brought to them."

Don Galo, however, Caballero's clerk, is a favourable specimen of his class; but a character that does not exist out of Spain.

The Carnival begins to-morrow; but it is not expected to be a very gay one, as we are still in a state of siege, and there have been so many regulations published about what characters may be personated and what may not. Religious orders are never allowed to be represented by the maskers, and this year it is forbidden to personate any public characters. If it had not been for this decree, I believe more than one representative of foreign Powers would have been seen stalking about the Prado, and a well-known lady who was very closely connected with one of them not long ago.

The shopkeepers say they are nearly ruined, and

it is no wonder, for, with the cholera first, and the insurrection after, a complete stop has been put to all gaiety, and there has been no "season" in Madrid this year at all. Not that it is ever a very gay place; but there are generally two or three balls given by some of the great people, and perhaps one or two at the Palace; but this winter there has not been one. Indeed, many people had not returned from their flight from the cholera when the insurrection broke out, and then, of course, they remained away, so that Madrid has looked quite deserted and miserable.

LETTER XVI.

Madrid, *February* 20, 1866.

The Carnival went off better than was expected; we had most beautiful weather, and that always makes a great difference, for the Spaniards will scarcely venture out if it is at all cold. Some of the masks were very good, and the people looked rather livelier than they did at the last Carnival I saw here. The masks that amused me most were a party of four gentlemen, who were got up as sportsmen and dogs. I do not know if I ever told you of the style in which the Spaniards go out for a day's shooting, but it has amused us many a time. First of all, they get themselves up in an elaborate costume of knickerbockers and boots, as if there were no end of ditches and hedges to get over; then, over their shoulders, they have about a

HOW DON JUAN GOES OUT SHOOTING.

dozen leather straps, crossing each other in every direction: to these are hung powder-flasks, and brandy-flasks, game-bags, and luncheon-cases, a huge brass horn, and a cage of call-birds, besides a number of other things, which I could not enumerate; suffice it to say, that you can scarcely see the sportsman for his traps. Thus equipped, Don Juan starts off, followed by a little boy carrying more effects, and another cage or two of call-birds. Once outside of Madrid, he sets to business. If he is of

DON JUAN IN AMBUSH.

such a grand order of sportsmen as to aspire to shoot partridges, he lets out his call-bird, which he fastens by the leg, and then hanging his cloak over two sticks fixed in the ground, he sits behind it until the unsuspecting birds come near enough to him, and then fires at them; but in a general way less noble game suffices him—he stalks larks! And we have often had a good laugh at him when, after carefully following them up for two or three fields' length, we have suddenly put an end to his little game by galloping past, and raising the birds. Sometimes he ensconces himself behind a large

THE GAME.

stone, and lies in wait there, having previously fastened a number of poor little larks by the leg, in different parts of the ground in front of him, as decoys, or set up a piece of looking-glass, or a revolving crescent of polished brass, which seems equally efficacious in attracting his prey. I must not forget his dog, which is of no particular breed, or use either, but which makes him look decidedly more dignified.

Two of the gentlemen I mentioned were got up as sportsmen, with an innumerable number of straps and dependent knick-knacks, including cages of live birds; they had long, white, miserable-looking masks on, and steeple-crowned hats of white felt. They first appeared riding two very small donkeys, and leading their dogs by a long, coloured cord. But I must describe the dogs, for they were the best part of the performance. One man was capitally got up as a shaved white poodle, with flannel trousers and jersey on, and ruffs of sheepskin round his arms and legs; his body was covered with sheepskin, and a long tail, which he kept splendidly cocked, was shaved down to the tip and left with a bushy end. A large dog's head rested on his shoulders, which made him appear about seven feet high; and round his neck was a broad blue ribbon with a cord attached, by which his master, who looked about half his size, led him.

The other dog was black, but shaved like his companion, and with a scarlet instead of a blue bow; his tail was left bushy and appeared to have a piece of thin elastic fastened to it which passed round his neck, for whenever he moved, it wagged in the most amiable way. You have no idea how extremely absurd this cavalcade looked coming solemnly down the Prado; but after a short time the donkeys were discarded, as they seemed to go too fast for the dogs, and the sportsmen continued their way on foot. Occasionally one of the dogs would make a point at a carriage where some pretty girl was sitting and would dash off after it, while the disconsolate master would crack his whip and utter melancholy groans on his big brass horn, to which, of course, the poodle paid no sort of attention. Sometimes the dogs would politely hand their cords to some lady; and I saw the white one running behind a mail-phaeton to which a very pretty girl had mischievously tied him, until, by a desperate effort, he managed to climb up into the back seat where she was, and make himself very comfortable by her side.

This party was said to be English, and, certainly, only English people could properly appreciate the satire.

I think we shall most probably leave for England in April or the beginning of May; we have not yet decided what route we shall take, but I think it will probably be Barcelona and Perpignan.

April 3, 1866.

We have been going through all sorts of religious duties lately, quite like good Catholics. On Thursday in the Holy Week, as I told you before, I think, no carriages or horses are allowed to go about within the gates of Madrid. The churches are hung with black, and the altars are illuminated, and the proper thing for the faithful to do is to visit as many churches as possible; seven is the lowest number allowable, but the more the better.

Accordingly, last Thursday we started, as well as the rest of the people, to pay our round of pious visits. We found the streets crowded to excess, and all the ladies dressed as for a *fête* and many of them carrying bouquets. At all the churches Civil Guards were posted, who obliged the people to pass in by one door and out by another, and a constant stream was kept up apparently for many hours. We went through six, but did not feel inclined to "do" another, even at the risk of losing all our labour by falling short of the orthodox number. No worship of any kind seemed to be performed, unless this passage through the church may be so called; and, as during these three days there is no sacrament on the altar, no reverence is necessary. Many of the altars were very prettily illuminated, especially one belonging to the Knights of St. John. In our search after churches we went to a part of Madrid I had never been in before. It stands very high, overlooking the Palace and, indeed, almost the whole of the city, and is evidently the oldest part, for the houses are large and handsome, with carved stone-facings and arms over the gateways; they appear to have been residences of the grandees, but they are now closed up and deserted; and, indeed, the whole place has a neglected air, though it is infinitely the best situation in Madrid. Almost at the summit of this hill stands the old church of San Andrés, and on the square tower a pair of storks have their nests; we watched them for a long time as they took their flight down over the valley of the Manzanares, which lay so far below, and back again to the airy pinnacle. The view is very fine from this point, for the descent to the river-side is so extremely precipitous that you seem to be hanging in the air and can see along the whole valley as far as the Pardo—a well-wooded property of the Queen, where she has a summer palace. If the country were only wooded or properly cultivated nearer Madrid, the view would be really superb; but now it is so barren and arid that it has a very dreary look. In one of the churches here we saw some most beautiful old tapestry, but I became so confused with the number we saw that day that I cannot remember which it was. Towards afternoon all the people who had finished their visitations congregated in the Carera San Gerónimo, where they paced up and down to see and be seen. The streets seemed so curiously quiet without any carriages, and the roadway all filled with foot-passengers; in the Puerta del Sol a number of officers had brought out chairs, and were sitting quietly smoking and criticizing the passers-by on the pavement before the office of the Government,—altogether it was evidently the great show-day of the year. I asked how it was that in Lent, and on the very eve of Good Friday, ladies were allowed to appear in such brilliant colours instead of the usual black, and the answer amused me excessively. It was because on that day Pilate made Christ put on the purple robe that good Catholics are also permitted to array themselves gorgeously.

The following day (Good Friday) we had agreed to go to Toledo to see the processions, and lionize the city; and accordingly we started about half-past six in the morning, that being the only train to be had. Our party consisted of four—three gentlemen and myself,—and we took the precaution of providing ourselves with breakfast, as we knew we could not quite trust to getting any at Toledo. On our way, the train made one of its usual long stoppages at a little village, and there we saw one of the most extraordinary scenes being enacted. I told you that in Spanish villages which are too poor to provide wooden images for their religious performances, living people personate the different characters; but I had never seen any take the part of Christ. In this rude village, however, the whole scene of the Crucifixion was represented in the little square in front of the church, which was also close to the railway station, so that we had a full view of the tableau. In the centre was a large wooden cross, and fastened on to it, to appear as if crucified, was a man. His arms were tied to the cross-beams, and, half-way down the cross, a wooden stool was fastened, so that he was actually kneeling on it, with his feet sticking out behind the cross; there was, therefore, no weight on his arms, but the position must have been a painful one. His head was bowed upon his breast, and I think he had on a crown of thorns, but we could not quite see whether it was so or not; he had on the old tattered brown cloth cloak which all the villagers wear hereabouts, and you cannot conceive what a melancholy parody the whole thing was. In front of the cross several lanterns were fixed on sticks into the ground, and the ladder, sponge, etc., were lying around. The villagers were devoutly kneeling, in humble adoration, before this poor wretch, who looked infinitely squalid and commonplace in his high position. We wondered whether he was a sinner, who was thus allowed to expiate his crimes, or if he were merely a very devout Catholic, and performed the duty of his own free will.

Toledo is a most interesting old place, and its position is the most commanding one you could conceive. It is built, as I dare say you remember from the photographs, on a hill, which rises suddenly from a vast plain, and below it the Tagus rushes along through rocky and precipitous banks, a narrow, but, when we saw it, an impetuous and turbid stream. As you approach the city from the railway station, you cross the river on a curious old bridge, leaving behind you another peaked hill, which is a counterpart to that on which Toledo is built, and which is crowned by the ruins of the ancient castle of Roderick, the last of the Gothic kings. After crossing the bridge, the road winds round the base of the hill, and a sharp turn brings you to the old Puerta del Sol, with its graceful horseshoe-arch. You have, however, still a pretty sharp ascent before you find yourself in the town itself, which is as curious as you can well imagine, with its narrow, badly-paved streets and its gorgeous remains of Moorish architecture. We went at once to the one hotel of the place, but an English party (who had come by the same train as we had, but had gone up to the town by an omnibus, instead of walking, as we had done) were beforehand with us, and had engaged the only rooms there were. This was a disappointment, for we had hoped to be able to watch the procession—the great event of the day—comfortably from a window, instead of mingling in the crowd. However, there was no help for it, so we started off to the cathedral, where we spent several hours. You have heard so much of it, and seen so many photographs, that I need not describe this noble old building; it is enough to say that it more than answered all my expectations. It was, of course, all darkened, being Good Friday, and only the altar was illuminated, and a large cross, formed entirely of small lamps, which was suspended in mid-air in the nave. After thoroughly examining and admiring the cathedral, we made our way up to the Alcázar, which crowns the apex of the hill and overlooks the wide plains and the narrow and rocky valley through which the Tagus winds almost in a circle round the city. There is but little left of this Alcázar, and what there is is Spanish rather than Moorish. Only the four outside walls remain, enclosing a large grass-grown court; but behind, a part of the building has been restored and is used as artillery barracks. We had intended to spend some time in the gardens of the palace while the gentlemen smoked, and enjoy the splendid view, but the gardens of which we had heard so much, proved to be merely a narrow strip of ground in front of the Alcázar and skirting the edge of the rock on which it stands. There was nothing very tempting about them, and there was a cold wind which howled about the empty walls, and seemed to threaten to hurl us down into the Tagus, which was boiling over its rocky bed immediately below us; so we were glad to come down again and find a more sheltered spot. We next went to see the Church of San Juan de los Reyes, going first into the museum, which is close by it, where we were shown the rooms of Cardinal Ximenes, now transformed into a picture-gallery.

This Church of San Juan was built by Ferdinand and Isabella to celebrate their triumph over the Moors; and a most noble monument it is, only I wish they never had conquered the Moors. It stands on one edge of a broad-topped hill, overhanging the plain below, through which the river winds like a silver thread. The architecture is most beautiful inside and out; the pillars are each different and are exquisitely carved; but what charmed us the most were the cloisters. Here we felt inclined to stay all day, and, indeed, we remained so long sitting on the benches, enjoying the quiet beauty of the scene, that the old man in charge kept toddling in every half-hour to see if we were in mischief. Every arch is ornamented with exquisite carvings of flowers and creepers. On one is a passion-flower, and no two leaves are alike; on another, a vine or climbing rose. This carving must have been a labour of love, for every little leaf and stalk represented is finished with the utmost perfection and truth; and you have no conception how beautiful these graceful arches, with their delicate tracery, looked with the sunlight shining through them, and the quadrangle filled with a wealth of luxuriant flowers and creepers behind. One of these, a white rose, had wound itself round one of the arches, and seemed to challenge comparison with its stone sister, as it waved about in the gentle breeze and shed its white blossoms on the floor of the cloister. Outside, the church is not less beautiful, and the most curious part of it is the ornamentation. In the grooves of the columns at the west end are hung long iron chains; and a portion of the wall over the great door, and also at the side of the church, is decorated with manacles. These are the actual chains that were taken off the Christians who were left in captivity by the Moors when they were expelled from Toledo. When the church was built they were hung up as offerings of gratitude, and, originally, I believe, the whole of the outside of the building was decorated in this way; indeed, you can still see the iron hooks which supported them, and the spaces on the walls which have been left bare by their removal. But when the French were in the country they carried off the greater part of these interesting relics, and sold them as old iron! It was late in the afternoon when we at last tore ourselves away from the beautiful cloisters, and having paid a visit to the curious little synagogue which, during the Moorish domination, the Jews

PRIEST.

were allowed to retain, we made our way back to the hotel and found the streets closely packed with the crowd waiting for the great procession. We were rather tired, and did not feel inclined to be pushed about by the rabble in the street; so we determined to give up all idea of seeing the procession, and go and have our dinner quietly in the hotel,—not without a little envy of the English people who had seized upon the only available windows.

I made a sketch of a priest in one of the old-fashioned "gimlets," which seem now to be giving place to narrower-brimmed hats, something similar to those worn by the French clergy.

We were sitting, waiting very patiently for our meal, when we heard the band strike up outside, and found the procession was being formed just outside the hotel. The English party had not come in yet, and, finding that the servants of the establishment were taking their places in the windows, we thought we might as well do the same, being quite prepared to vacate our positions as soon as the owners appeared. But one glance at the tightly-packed crowd beneath convinced us that, if they had not already entered the hotel, there was not the faintest chance of their ever doing so until the procession had passed, and we should have the benefit of their windows all to ourselves; so we made ourselves quite comfortable and had a capital view of the whole performance. First came some lugubrious-looking individuals dressed from head to foot in black calico, with nothing more than holes for their eyes; no face or, indeed, head visible. Then came the Captain-General, and a number of other "swells" in full-dress uniform, walking two-and-two, each carrying a long lighted candle. Every now-and-then came one of the black demons,—for they looked like nothing else,—carrying a kind of huge quiver filled with candles for the use of any private individual who was pious enough to follow in the procession; next came the band, and then the officers, and, finally, the men of the artillery quartered in the town. The young officers seemed rather ashamed of their duty, and amused themselves by winking at the girls in the crowd, and trying to drop as much tallow as possible over every one they passed. Sometimes they would extinguish their candle altogether by poking it at the back of the unfortunate comrade who happened to be in front of them, at the same time keeping a sharp look-out behind that no one was playing the same trick on them. After these came a file of black demons, and then a large platform carried by more demons, on which was a lifesize figure of the Virgin, dressed in black velvet, with an extensive crinoline and a long train; she had a tiara of diamonds on, and bracelets and necklace of the same. After her came a number of Roman soldiers in armour, the two last trailing banners in the dirt; and then another platform with a figure of Christ on the cross, life-size, and with the four Marys weeping at the foot. This was necessarily a very large affair, and required a great number of men to carry it. The next scene was the taking down from the cross, and contained a great many figures; the body was unfastened from the cross, and was being lowered down by a man who stood upon a ladder placed against the back of the cross, and leaned over, holding the long cloth which supported the body; below were three or four men receiving it. All these figures were beautifully executed;—there was no wooden appearance about them. Lastly came the body, laid in a glass coffin; it was covered with flowers and the crown of thorns was laid on the top, where the chaplet is generally placed,—a few more Roman soldiers closed the procession.

It was a painful sight; the people all went down on their knees as their wooden gods went by, tumbling and reeling as the black familiars who carried them tripped over the uneven pavement. I can always kneel at the elevation of the Host, and bow on passing the altars with becoming reverence; but I could not bring myself to bow before these idols, even though I might shock the religious feelings of the people who were round me by not doing so, there was something so gross in this fetish worship. You frequently hear the people disputing about the respective powers and efficacy of their particular image, the inhabitants of Zaragoza lauding their celebrated Vírgen del Pilar over that of the Atocha, and the Madrileños upholding the dignity of their little black idol.

After the procession had passed, and we were thinking of returning to our deserted dinner-table, we saw the English people, whose room we had benefited by, vainly struggling to reach the hotel through the crowd below. It was just where four narrow streets met, and the people, all trying to go different ways, formed a perfect whirlpool in the middle, where the two young ladies were being hopelessly twisted round and round, while the two gentlemen and the courier who were with them seemed powerless to assist them. We were very sorry for them,—but we had enjoyed the use of their windows very much.

After dinner we went to the cathedral again, and sat in the cloisters; the priests were making ready for a great resurrection-scene to be enacted the next morning at the rending of the veil. The illuminated cross was lowered, and its lamps blown out: then it disappeared through a trap-door to wait until next Good Friday. In the nave there was erected an immense flight of imitation white marble steps, and at the top was the sepulchre; men were bringing in the angels and archangels on stretchers, wings uppermost, and placing them on the steps, in readiness for the morrow. One of our party made his way into the green-room, where these dignitaries were being taken out of their baize covers and made ready for the performance. After remaining some time in the cathedral, we walked down towards the station, stopping, however, after crossing the river, to climb the hill where the ruins of the old Gothic castle stand. We sat on the grass, among the ruins, admiring the splendid view, until we had only just time to reach the station, and catch the train for Madrid.

Coming to Toledo in the morning, we had changed carriages at a little place called Castellejos, and were told we should have to do the same on our return in the evening. Accordingly, as soon as we arrived at the station, we prepared to make a rush for a carriage, as the train from Alicante, which we were to join, is always very full. It was quite dark, the station being only lighted by an oil lamp. To make matters worse, our portion of the train was not near the station, so we had to jump out where we were, and found we had a wall about five feet high to climb to reach the platform: by help of the luncheon-basket, which formed a step, and the efforts of the gentlemen, however, I scrambled up, being much relieved to find the other English ladies were in the same predicament. All the passengers were making a rush, and we followed them; and not seeing the Alicante train before us, the whole body scampered down the platform, and turning round the corner of a building came upon the train, standing empty; we were preparing to take our seats, when some one discovered it was the same we had just left;—we had merely made a circular *détour*, and come back to the same place. It was too absurd: the only consolation was that everybody was alike. We asked where our train was, and the guard told us it had not come up from Alicante: he further informed us we had better go back to our carriages, as we might not have to change at all; it would depend on the number of passengers in the train from the south. So the wall had to be jumped again; but we had scarcely seated ourselves in the carriage before the other train came up, and one of our party, who had remained on the platform to get the earliest information, called out to us that we were to change, and immediately rushed off to secure seats. We followed as quickly as the difficulties of wall-climbing would allow us, and only just managed to get into the carriage he was guarding for us, when there was a terrific rush, and every seat was filled; then ensued a most amusing scene—amusing for us, at least, who could afford to laugh. There were twice as many passengers as there were seats, and after half an hour of shouting, screaming, and rushing frantically about, on the part of the unfortunate passengers who were *de trop*, we quietly started for Madrid, leaving the station quite full of desperate and gesticulating people, who had paid for their places, but were very composedly left behind by the officials. I imagine they would have to pass the night at Castellejos, for the railway people did not seem to have the slightest intention of sending them on, nor did they make use of the carriages which had come from Toledo, for some unexplained reason.

We did not feel inclined to go through any more religious duties the next day, so we started off early in the morning to spend the day at the Pardo. Several friends, who were staying in Madrid, joined us, so we formed quite a large party. Some of the gentlemen and Henry and

I rode, and the others drove. It was a lovely day, and we had a most enjoyable excursion. The road is bordered with trees the whole way to the Pardo, which lies about eight miles from Madrid, on the banks of the Manzanares, and for the greater portion of the way there is a stretch of common, with good turf and plenty of trees, between the road and the river; so that we had a splendid ride on grass almost the whole way, and, as the late rains have made everything spring up wonderfully, it was really grass, and not scorched stubble.

We did not see the palace, or indeed look for it, but spent the day in the park, which looks pretty and green, and the trees, being almost all ilex, and therefore covered with leaves, gave it quite the appearance of summer; indeed, we were very glad to sit in the shade to eat our luncheon, for it was an exceedingly hot day. The river looked quite imposing, considering it was the Manzanares, for it was very full, and rolled along in a pompous manner, as if proud of having so much water to boast of. It was about as wide as the Thames at Cliefden, and formed a very pretty feature in the landscape. But the ride home was what I enjoyed the most: we started just as the full moon was rising in a cloudless sky, and you can have no idea how beautiful the place looked in her brilliant light; the shadows were so deep, and the river seemed like liquid silver, winding between its grassy banks; the air was filled with the cry of innumerable *cigarras* (grasshoppers) and frogs, and a most musical sound it was, though we are not accustomed to consider a frog a melodious creature, and speak of his "croaking;" but I do not know why, for his call has certainly nothing hoarse about it, and, when you hear a number of them together, they have a shrill, bell-like sound. Every now and then would come the whit-too-hoo of an owl from one of the trees. Henry said it was exactly like a night in a Brazilian forest; it was like nothing I had ever seen or heard before, and I enjoyed it immensely. Then, rightly or wrongly, there is always a feeling of possible danger in riding outside Madrid at night—Spaniards would not do it for the world,—so we felt delightfully bogyish as we rode along, with the cool night air whistling past us, and the shadows of the trees seemed to take all sorts of strange shapes.

We intend to pay one more visit to the Pardo before we leave for England. One great advantage of this ride is that we can go for some distance through the Florida, which I think I told you was a nicely-planted estate of the King's, with a good avenue of trees, about two miles long. You must remember that in speaking of these wooded places, I do not mean that they are pretty, as compared with any English park or country road, for the trees are generally small and sickly-looking, and it is only in spring that there is any grass to be seen or any water in the river; but it is so much here to see even the semblance of a tree that we learn to think any place beautiful where they are to be found.

This road to the Pardo, however, would bear comparison with any English one, for the trees are really fine along the riverside, and the ground on each side undulates prettily. I fancy that visitors to Madrid seldom see this, its best side, for, as

Spaniards do not care for country beauty, they would never dream of directing any one to it.

I think we shall start about the 12th or 14th, and intend going by Valencia, Taragona, and Barcelona, and across the Pyrenees, by diligence, to

DONKEY CARRYING STRAW.

Perpignan. I shall write again, however, before we leave.

I send you a sketch of some of the objects we meet in our country rides. I give both a side and back elevation of the animal, for fear you should not otherwise be able to recognize it.

LETTER XVII.

Perpignan, *April* 24, 1866.

We left Madrid, as we intended, on the 14th, and arrived in Valencia the next morning. Nothing very particular happened on our journey, except that in the middle of the night,—that is to say, about one o'clock in the morning,—just as we had been congratulating ourselves on getting rid of two fellow-passengers and having the carriage to ourselves, and had tucked ourselves up in our rugs and gone to sleep, the door was thrown open, and a gruff voice informed us that we were to change carriages. Henry asked the reason, as we had been told in Madrid that we should have no changes. It was because several passengers had got out, and by packing some of the carriages a little more closely it would be possible to leave one behind. So we were unceremoniously sent into a carriage where there were already six people,—and such people!

One of the most extraordinary things in Spanish railway travelling is the company you meet with in the first-class carriages. Who make use of the second and third I do not know, but certainly the ragamuffins who sometimes travel in the first would seem to be much better there. No one would ever dream of their being first-class passengers. Spaniards nearly always travel at night, and they set about it in a very business-like style. The ladies come to the station with woollen hoods over their head, and often wear a sort of loose dressing gown so that they are quite ready for sleep. The first thing the men do is to take off their boots and put on a pair of carpet slippers, then, rolling themselves up in their cloaks, head and all, they stretch themselves along the seat,—if there is room to do so,—and the soles of their slippers is all you see of them for the rest of the journey. If they could, they would shut up every window and ventilator quite close, but, fortunately, the corner passenger has the right to open the little side-window next himself; so that if you are at the station in time to secure one of these seats you can avoid being utterly stifled, but that is all. Sometimes your five or six fellow-passengers all smoke; but that I almost prefer, as, though the tobacco may not be very good, it drowns other smells. You know I can stand any amount of smoking, but those who cannot should certainly keep out of Spain, for you will never be asked if you like it or not; it is so much a matter of course, that a Spaniard lights his cigar just as composedly as an Englishman would open his newspaper.

We did not stay long in Valencia, as we had spent some time there on our last visit, and we passed along the pretty coast, where we had driven before, so rapidly that we could see none of its beauties. Part of the journey to Barcelona has to be performed by diligence, but as it is across the valley of the Ebro and the scenery is pretty, I was very glad of the variety. We had started at half-past four o'clock in the morning, by train, and neglected to take any provisions with us, thinking we should find some sort of refreshment station on our way. In this, however we were mistaken, for on reaching Amposta, where we took the diligence, we found there was nothing in the shape of food to be had. While we were waiting for the luggage to be packed Henry went off on a foraging expedition, and succeeded in discovering a little stall kept by an old woman for the benefit of the railway officials. From her he obtained two slices of very stale bread, and two little dry bones about the length of your first finger, which were called mutton-chops.

As we had only had a cup of chocolate before leaving Valencia, and it was then twelve o'clock, we were very glad of even this food, and gnawed our bones quite greedily. There was nothing on them, but still we had the glory of them; and it was all the food we got until we reached Barcelona, about half-past eight in the evening.

The drive across the Ebro was delicious. We

had seats in a sort of open *coupé* behind the driver, who was not perched up at the top of the coach as in the French diligences. There was a strong wind which carried off all the dust, so that we were not annoyed in that way, and Henry very wisely provided the driver with good cigars, so that we had, at least, respectable tobacco puffed into our faces.

As you descend the valley of the Ebro the scenery is very pretty. The country is well wooded, and there are comfortable, neat little homesteads about that look singularly un-Spanish. You cross the river, which is a fine, broad, rolling stream, on an antiquated bridge of boats which seems to be dropping to pieces, and enter the town of Tortosa, the strangest old place I ever saw. It seems very large, and is fortified; on one side the river washes the walls of the houses, which are all of the most ancient description; the streets are very narrow, and filthily dirty, nevertheless I should have very much liked to explore them a little, for they looked so curious.

We noticed such an extraordinary change in the

appearance of the people we passed on the road in this neighbourhood: they were mostly fair and with rosy cheeks, as you see among the country people in England, and the children were quite different from the shrivelled little monkeys you see in Castile.

When you join the railway again the line runs close along the seashore, and the country is flat and uninteresting. We had intended to stop a day at Taragona, but when we saw it we were very glad we had not arranged to do so. It seems to be a staring, new place, with rows of pretentious-looking lodging-houses, and we were told afterwards that there was nothing to be seen there.

With Barcelona, however, I was very much pleased; it is certainly at least a hundred years in advance of Madrid, and is more like a French than a Spanish town. It is prettily situated, and is surrounded by wooded hills, which are studded with pretty villas. Through the centre of the town runs the Rambla, a fine promenade well shaded with trees. The windows of our hotel looked on to this Rambla, as, indeed, all the best houses in Barcelona do, and it was a great amusement to sit in the balcony and watch the constant stream of passers-by. Under the trees, at the side are numbers of flower-stalls, and at one of these we bought a magnificent bouquet of tea-roses, and other flowers, for six reales, about fifteenpence. Early in the morning I used to see numbers of people buying flowers and taking them home, and I quite liked the Barcelonese for their taste, for the Castilians do not care an atom for flowers, and would not thank you for them if they had them. There are gardens on all sides in Barcelona, public and private, in which the flowers were most luxuriant, though it was only April. The trees on the Rambla are watered by an underground stream, which is turned on twice a day; they are very fine, and it is delicious to have this shady walk, instead of the hot, blazing pavement. A Spanish friend of Henry's, however, who was with us in Barcelona, told us it was never very hot there at any time, as there is always a breeze from the sea about twelve o'clock, which makes it cool and pleasant. A great many people live at

Gracia, a pleasant suburb, to which omnibuses ply constantly.

There are a great many interesting places in Barcelona, such as the cathedral, the old palace of the Counts of Barcelona, the Church of Santa Maria del Mar, and many others. We had intended also going up the fortress of Monguich, but we left it for our last afternoon, and some people came to call, and stayed so long that we were obliged to give it up; I was very sorry for this, as I had wished particularly to see the fortress. From below it seems so utterly impossible to take it by storm, and gives one a wonderful idea of Lord Peterborough's hot-headed valour.

We went twice to the opera, and heard 'Ernani' and 'Don Giovanni,' both capitally given. The theatre is one of the finest in Europe, I believe, and the scenery and all the arrangements were very good. We could not get a libretto containing the names of the singers, but all the parts were well taken, and the orchestra was well conducted. The whole thing was infinitely better done than in Madrid, where one set of scenery does for all the operas, and there are never more than one, or at most, two, good singers, and all the others are "sticks." In Barcelona there was a rival company giving operas in the other large theatre, but as the sisters Marchisio were performing there, we did not feel inclined to hear them again, having had quite enough of them in Madrid. We had a Spanish gentleman with us when we heard 'Don Giovanni,' who had never seen that opera before, and I was greatly amused with him in the last scene. When the commandant takes Don Juan away, he sinks through a trap-door, from which issue red flames and smoke; at the same time the scenery at the back divides and discloses a very warm place, in which are numbers of scarlet and black devils, dancing and leaping about in the midst of flames. When Don Juan appears by a side-door they all run to meet him, with signs of the greatest delight, and the curtain falls upon a scene of general rejoicing and merriment, which is certainly not calculated to act as a warning to the wicked. Our Spanish friend was charmed; he rubbed his hands, and said over and over again, "What amiable devils; how happy, how light-hearted, and how pleased to welcome Don Juan! I shall never forget them."

The crossing of the Pyrenees to Perpignan has to be done by diligence, and when Henry went to secure places he found, to his great dismay, that we could not get a *coupé*, except by waiting for several days, which we did not feel inclined to do; so we resigned ourselves, and determined to make the best of the corner seats in the interior. We left Barcelona at half-past four o'clock in the morning, and when we came downstairs in the cold grey dawn, we found our Spanish friend already waiting to accompany us to the station— imagine getting up at four o'clock in the morning, to see a friend off! He seemed as much impressed with Don Juan and his friends as on the previous evening, and we left him saying, "Que demónios, tan amables, tan alegres, paseandose!"

The line runs along the shore for some distance after you leave Barcelona, and the scenery is pretty, with the sea on one side and mountains on the other. Homely-looking little villages and gentlemen's houses, embowered in trees, stud these hills, and give one the idea that Barcelona might be a very pleasant place to live in. I was greatly struck with the appearance of the Catalans; they seem quite a different race from other Spaniards; indeed, you could scarcely recognize them as Spaniards at all. They are taller and better made, and are, many of them, fair, with an aquiline nose, and a high, smooth forehead, very different to the low, narrow foreheads, seamed with longitudinal wrinkles, which you see among the people of the other provinces. The women, too, seemed to walk more gracefully, and were certainly much finer-looking than the celebrated Andaluzas or Gaditanas. Barcelona is so much in advance of other Spanish towns, and the Catalans have so much more enterprise than the majority of their countrymen, that one cannot help wondering that they and the Basques, who are also a very fine race, have not together regenerated the rest of Spain, or, at least, obtained a decided ascendancy over it.

When we reached Gerona, where our diligence

journey began, we found we had to wait for about an hour, during which time breakfast was provided for the passengers at the inn from which we were to start. Remembering our experience in crossing the Ebro, we took advantage of this opportunity of eating, though the refreshments provided in the Spanish Fondas are none of the best. However, one can always get fowl, and that, at least, is tolerably free from garlic, and, though wonderfully lean, is eatable. The wine is less agreeable, being sometimes almost undrinkable, from the horrible taste of the pig-skin in which it is kept; but when one is thirsty, one can put up with almost anything; and this wine, which by itself tastes like bootvarnish, can be swallowed when plentifully diluted with water, and the water certainly cannot be drunk alone.

Breakfast over, we went downstairs to the diligence, which we found already packed. We at once took possession of our corner seats; the other two corners were already occupied by a very stout old lady and gentleman. The interior now seemed to be quite full, and we were, indeed, very closely packed; but, lo and behold! two gentlemen presented themselves as claimants of the centre seats, and prepared to make good their entrance. We squeezed ourselves into our corners, and the old couple squeezed themselves into theirs, but still there did not appear to be room for a baby, let alone for a man, on each side; and one of the new passengers was decidedly stout! However, the horses were in, and they must find places somewhere; so they climbed in over us by help of the straps at the top of the carriage, and sat down on our knees. We were really suffocated, but fortunately every one was in a good humour, and we hoped we should shake down by-and-by. In the meantime, I could not help wondering what we should do for pocket-handkerchiefs, for to get at our pockets was an utter impossibility. Just as we were starting, we found our side-windows, or rather shutters, would open, so Henry and I each put an arm outside, which relieved us wonderfully, and after half-an-hour's jolting and shaking, we really did settle down into some sort of shape,—but it was that of well-packed sardines.

I remembered how often I had proclaimed my preference for diligence over railway travelling, and modified my views a little. It was an exceedingly hot day, and the dust was flying in clouds, so our journey was not a very agreeable one, more especially as the horses were very slow, and we seemed to creep over the ground; the only good thing was that all the passengers were good-humoured, and made the best of their sufferings. We were much disappointed in the pass, which is very inferior to the other roads over the Pyrenees by which we had crossed, but something of that might be due to the circumstances under which it was seen. I found the repacking such a difficult business that I never left my seat, except at the French frontier, where our luggage was examined,—I was fortunate again, and my portmanteau was not even opened.

Just at the boundary between the two countries is the fortress Bellegarde, on a high peaked hill, which commands every turn of the road for miles; it is in a splendid position, and looks immensely strong. The road was very good, but some of the walls in the sharp turnings of the ravines were so broken, and in some places altogether gone, that I felt glad we were crossing by daylight instead of at night. Towards evening I alone remained awake, and watched the burning of a house, or

BULLOCK DRIVER IN WINTER.

some houses, far away in the mountains; I saw it from the first outburst of flames, until it sank at last into a sullen, red, smouldering fire. It seemed far away from any other habitation, and I wondered what would become of the poor occupants left houseless in the night.

We were thankful to reach Perpignan, and be unpacked, stiff and aching, with our arms almost broken, from being twisted round the window-frame so long; for the last hour I had slept with my head through the window too, so that my neck felt all awry as well.

Nevertheless, I could not resist sitting up long after I had gone to my room listening to the nightingales with which this place seems to swarm; they sang the whole night through, and were still singing this morning when we went for a stroll in the pretty promenade which lies just outside the town. Perpignan is not very pretty, because it is so flat; but it is buried in luxuriant gardens, which are delicious to the eye coming from Spain.

We leave to-morrow for Geneva, from whence I expect my next letter will be dated.

LETTER FROM AN EYEWITNESS OF THE INSURRECTION, JUNE 22, 1866.

ANNEXED is a letter written by a friend who was in Madrid during the insurrection of the 22nd of June, 1866. It will be remembered that after crushing this attempt at a revolution—the most serious one that has taken place for some years,—O'Donnell was virtually made dictator, as a decree passed the Cortes and Senado suspending the constitutional guarantees; but within a few days he was ousted from the cabinet by a backstairs intrigue, and Narvaez took his place and inaugurated the "reign of terror" which has ever since existed. Narvaez was wounded in the shoulder, or pretended to be so, in the affair of the 22nd June, and was carried into the Palace, and it was believed in Madrid that he took that opportunity of arranging with the Queen the dismissal of the Duke of Tetuan and his own elevation to the premiership. It was said—I do not know with what truth—that O'Donnell heard something of the intrigue and went to the Queen, representing to her that if it were true he was to be required to resign, it was useless to go on shooting the insurgents who were then under sentence of death, since under a new minister they might be pardoned. Isabel, however, assured him that there was no foundation for the report; that he must continue to hold his office; and the daily execution of the revolted troops went on.

In a day or two the intrigue was brought to a successful issue, and O'Donnell retired both from the Ministry and from Spain, vowing that he would never take office again so long as Isabel Segunda was on the throne.

MADRID, *June 22nd*, 1866.

MY DEAR,—At last, after an immensity of talking, the revolution has commenced. Old Canuto woke me up at eight o'clock this morning, with a broad grin upon his face, to tell me the news.

I jumped up and looked out; sure enough, there were piquets of troops all down the Prado, and a strong body of cavalry massed near the fountain at the entrance of the Calle Alcalá. Dropping shots, mixed now and then with the platoon firing of the troops, came from the direction of the Puerta del Sol. According to Canuto, the affair began about four o'clock in the morning with the revolt of a regiment of artillery in the large, new, red barracks near the Palace, just above the Northern Railway Station. Prim is stated to be in command, but with what truth I do not know.

When I got downstairs I found a piquet of cavalry stationed at the end of the street leading into the Prado, and the usual number of heads peering out from all the balconies. From this side of the house we heard no firing, and, with the exception of the troops, everything appeared much as usual.

About ten, Alison came in and reported the Puerta del Sol to be full of troops, as also the Calle

Alcalá; cannon pointed up the streets, but no fighting going on; he met two wounded officers limping home. According to his account, the fighting is now going on in the Plazuela Santo Domingo and the Calle Ancha San Bernardo, which you will recollect.

11 A.M.—Canuto has just returned from a reconnaissance; he reports a large barricade building in the Calle del Prado, near the statue of Cervantes. The insurgents caught him and wanted him to assist, but, as he knew the chief of the barricade, he got off.

12 M.—After another reconnaissance Canuto reports the Plazuela Anton Martin, at the top of the Calle Atocha, where there is a fountain with four dolphins, as being turned into a regular fortress; the entrance from the Calle Leon and all the other streets strongly barricaded. No fighting going on; the people in this part of the town, so far, have it all their own way. As for me, I cannot get up sufficient interest in their aimless insurrections to make me feel inclined to risk my life in cruising about the streets for nothing, and so remain ingloriously at home.

1 P.M.—We have just finished a good breakfast, —I suppose the last fresh meat we shall get for some time. Canuto says we can do very well for seven or eight days, as we have two hams and a sack of rice in the house. The firing still continues on the north side; a large force of artillery, cavalry, and infantry, have just gone up the Calle Alcalá towards the Puerta del Sol.

4 P.M.—Canuto has returned from another expedition; he has been to a barricade in the Calle San Juan, where another of his numerous friends is commanding. He was told that the Plazuela de Anton Martin had been taken by the troops; but that is scarcely probable, as we should have heard the firing very distinctly if such had been the case.

A body of artillery and cavalry have gone up the Carrera San Gerónimo, and another down the Prado; they are probably going to make a combined movement on the Plazuela Anton Martin,— one party going up the Calle Leon, and the other up the Calle Atocha.

5 P.M.—Canuto reports another barricade in the

Plaza de Jésus, at the top of the Lope de Vega. Artillery seems to be flying about in every direction, but I hear no firing now; perhaps they are taking up position for a general attack. It is said numbers of the troops will desert to-night. *Quien sabe?*

Firing has recommenced with vigour all round, chiefly from the Puerta del Sol and the Calle Atocha; now and then we hear the loud boom of a cannon, mixed with the sharp, quick peal of musketry.

7 P.M.—All sounds of firing have ceased. Canuto has just turned up again, and reports several new barricades; but in all those near us there seems to be no fighting. Prim is reported to have given orders that they shall not be defended at present. When the troops come up, the people fire a few shots and retire; the troops knock down the barricade and go on; as soon as they have left, the people return and rebuild it. I suppose they intend to offer this kind of passive resistance for a day or two, in order to wait the effect the rising here may cause in the provinces.

It appears that the regiment that "pronounced" this morning has sixteen pieces of artillery; it is reported to have had a fight with the troops for a couple of hours, and to have retired to the new barracks I told you of, which have been fortified. I think I shall take a little cruise into the town, and see how things are going on.

7.30 P.M.—I believe the whole thing is a "jolly sell," as usual a true " Cosa de España." I have been up and examined several of the so-called barricades—wretched, miserable things, not worthy of the name, about four feet high. I went up to the Plazuela Anton Martin, where they were best defended, and asked some of the people who were crowding about the doors. It appears there were only two or three dozen men, who employed themselves all day in firing down the streets at any soldier who chanced to present himself. About 5.30, when I heard the most vigorous firing, all the barricades were taken by assault, about half-a-dozen killed and wounded representing the total loss. If this is all "nuestros valientes" can do, the sooner they emigrate to Congo-land the better.

THE REVOLUTION AT AN END. 317

I should have no objection to meet 10,000 Spaniards at the head of 1000 English. All the barricades are now abandoned; it is reported that the fighting is to commence again this evening; it is to be hoped, for the honour of Spain, it will, for I can compare this, so far, to nothing but a " barring out" at school.

10.30 P.M.—All quiet; not a soul in the streets. I am afraid the whole thing is going to be a gigantic "sell." "Veremos,"—if nothing takes place during the night, to-morrow everything will be in its usual condition, and O'Donnell will begin his "fusilamientos" in the Fuente Castellano, and add a few more scalps to those which already decorate his wigwam.

June 23.—It is all over, and the Revolution at an end, at any rate for the present. I have just come in from a cruise round the principal points of defence; the town is still occupied by troops, a regiment of infantry camped out in front of the Cortes, lying asleep on their arms in every direction about the footpaths. I suppose they have been there all night. The Puerta del Sol is very strongly occupied by mounted artillery and infantry. Here the soldiers would not let me pass, so I turned across the Calle Sevilla, and crossed the Calle Alcalá into the Caballero de Gracia; all these streets were lined with piquets of soldiers, under arms. From the Caballero de Gracia, I got up to the top of the Calle Montera, where is the fountain with tortoises; here was a strong force of infantry and artillery; the guns pointed down the Calle Fuencarral, and the gunners asleep on the guns. From here I went through a number of by-streets, all barricaded, and bearing traces of the recent fight, in broken furniture, pools of blood—which men were busy washing away with the water-jets—houses pitted with balls, doors smashed in, etc. etc., and so gained the Calle Ancha San Bernardo, and the Plaza Santo Domingo. Here the fight had been hottest; the houses were all thickly pitted with shot and cannon marks, and doors and windows smashed.

On my way I called on our friend Señora Fuentes, whose son, you know, is in the artillery. She had, as you may imagine, spent a miserable day and night. Her son's regiment was the first to pronounce; they shot their colonel, and disarmed the other officers, but did not shoot any of them. Francisco, however, was made prisoner by the insurgents, and his life was only spared by the sergeant of his own company. This regiment was joined by a regiment of cazadores, and, after some fighting in the streets, they are reported to have gone off into the country. It is certain that a number of troops have been sent out this morning, I suppose in pursuit.

In going along the streets, I met now and then wounded and dead men being carried to the hospitals, as well as people going to deliver up arms, as an edict has been issued commanding all arms to be given up within eight hours, under pain of death. The revolution here is, I should say, successfully crushed; it appears to have been badly managed; the people were very short of arms and ammunition, their positions and barricades badly chosen and constructed, and to have held out so long, only because the troops, instead of charging, contented themselves with taking pot-shots round the corners from a long distance,—whenever they charged, the barricades were abandoned at once.

For the present all is over here. If it be true, as they say, that Valladolid and other towns have pronounced, it may not end yet, as the flame may spread, and O'Donnell cannot afford to send many troops away from Madrid. At present paviors are busy repairing the streets, and cleaning away the blood; no business, of course, is doing.

I am afraid that, objectless as the whole thing appears, many lives have been lost. It is reported that General Serrano, Duque de la Torre, is killed, and Narvaez wounded; but, of course, as yet, no reliable information is to be had.

June 25.

The affair was more serious than I thought. The regiments that pronounced were the horse and foot artillery, about 13,000 strong, with thirty guns. They were joined by a number of common people. The great fight was at the new barracks near the Palace. Many of the officers were shot down at the first rising. The total number of killed and wounded on the side of the troops is 500, including seven General officers; of the people, no list is given,—it will not be so heavy as that of the troops. The loss among the officers has been very heavy.

For the present the insurrection may be said to be crushed, so I will finish my letter, which I had expected to be much longer. My hams are not cut into yet; they will do for next revolution.

THE END.

J. E. TAYLOR AND CO., PRINTERS, LITTLE QUEEN STREET, HOLBORN.

www.ingramcontent.com/pod-product-compliance
Lightning Source LLC
Chambersburg PA
CBHW021206230426
43667CB00006B/587